TABLE OF

PREFACE

My midlife crisis had been growing steadily more acute for the past three or four years, when, aged forty-four, I hit rock bottom. Actually, that's not true — there was no "rock bottom" as such. There was no impulsive divorce or affair with a twenty-three-year-old receptionist. No staying in bed for days on end or rocking back and forth with my head between my legs. No middle-finger sign off to a bewildered boss or road trip across America on a Harley Davidson.

While these are the cliché actions associated with midlife crisis in men, they're by no means the predominant ones. The vast majority of men, like me, suffer in silence. Being the less communicative of the two genders, us guys tend to keep our problems bottled up rather than offload them on our partners, family members or hairdressers. But this is where problems can arise, as pent up thoughts and emotions usually end up doing one of two things: 1. Finally erupt as a midlife crisis cliché in the form of an affair, divorce or sudden resignation, 2. Stay suppressed but generate increasing amounts of regret, resentment, anger and unhappiness until the sufferer gives up and emotionally "dies" inside.

In my case, I was on course to do the latter as a continual daily stream of negative thoughts about my past, present and future gradually began to overwhelm my day to day existence.

Some of these may be familiar to you:

- "Why didn't I do X instead of Y twenty years ago?"
- "Is *this* all there is?"
- "You think you look bad now, just give it another ten years."
- "I can feel the cold hand of Death on my shoulder."
- "What's the point of anything?"
- "I wish I was twenty-one again."
- "Women don't even look at me anymore."
- "I need to change something, but I don't know what."

Why exactly I was suffering from a midlife crisis, I probably couldn't articulate if you'd asked me. I was married and enjoyed the company of a few good friends. I was self-employed and made okay money. I was yet to experience any major health issues or tragedies in my life. Generally, you could say I led a pretty privileged and comfortable existence, certainly when compared with many others less fortunate in the world.

All I knew, however, was that my life hadn't quite turned out as I'd expected it to, or wanted it to for that matter. I hadn't led the mind-blowing, spectacular life I'd envisaged as a twenty-one-year-old fresh out of university and ready to take on the world. Instead of taking on the world, I'd I shrunk away from it. All my youthful hopes and dreams had slowly dissipated one by one until I was left with the day to day existence of merely striving to make money. But for what? The crushing sensation that I'd wasted my life pressed down upon me from the moment I opened my eyes every morning, to the moment I closed them again at night.

As you've purchased this book, the chances are you're going through a similar form of crushing ennui and feeling of hopelessness caused by a male midlife crisis that I went through. Maybe you've asked for help and been told "There's nothing you can do but just get on with life", "It's not really a midlife crisis", "Get over it", and so on. As well-intentioned as these nuggets of wisdom are, they're of little use to a midlife crisis sufferer. Intellectually you know you they're right — you should just "get over it" — but how?

Well, this is precisely the purpose of this book — to show you how to do just that. While everyone's experiences and problems will be different, the means of getting over them are universal.

In all the time I was plagued by my midlife crisis and searching for the answer, *something was working*... My mind was taking on board a substantial amount of information as I searched, often by looking deep within myself. As time went on I began to realize that certain positive thoughts, concepts, and most importantly, actions, seriously helped to quell negative midlife crisis feelings more than others, and herein lies the genesis of this book. I ended up focusing on several key concepts that really helped me to see my situation in a much clearer light. Within a couple of months these concepts — coupled with the daily practical exercises outlined throughout each step — had dramatically reduced the effects of my midlife crisis.

Some time afterwards I decided to write this book in order to help fellow sufferers regain control of their mind and life. However, it's not for guys who have an easily definable *reason* to be unhappy — those suffering from bereavement, a major illness, disability, depression or any other form of considerable life trauma. (Please consult with a professional if this is the case.) Rather, this book is for all of you who are suffering from the nebulous sensation that your life's a failure, without really knowing why and yet don't wish to wait three, five or ten years until it passes (if at all).

Although I can say with confidence that my midlife crisis is now over, let me stress that I have absolutely no qualifications or special skills to back up this book other than my direct experience. In other words, I'm not a psychologist or a doctor, but just a regular guy who has successfully squashed his midlife crisis after a long and protracted struggle — and ultimately by myself. Stick with the program, put in the work and you'll be able to rid yourself of these pointless, negative thoughts and emotions and kick your midlife crisis to the curb much quicker than I did.

INTRO

"If my mind can conceive it, and my heart can believe it, then I can achieve it."
– Muhammed Ali

Imagine for a moment, two ducks swimming in a lake. Everything's calm and peaceful. Then, one duck decides to attack the other duck. There's a flapping of wings, splashing of water and maybe some squawking, but just as suddenly as the conflict began, it's over. The two ducks swim away from each other like nothing happened. In this regard, people should be more like ducks. We should be able to brush off regrets, altercations, moods, thoughts and emotions and just get on with our day. But the majority of us find this extremely difficult. Whether it's remaining angry about an argument for days, or ruminating on a grudge, or obsessing over past mistakes, we humans love hanging on to things that we should probably just let go. This is the aim of this book: to enable you to let go of the constant stream of anxious thoughts and emotions you currently have about your life and defeat your midlife crisis.

How do we do this? We do it in twelve steps... Each step looks at an individual cause of your midlife crisis, say, ageism in society, and sets out to tackle it. I show you how to do this by rewiring the mind to think about the cause in a different light. Changing the way you think about certain concepts is an essential step on the road to overcoming a midlife crisis, but the mind will attempt to resist this at all costs unless it's backed up by action. And that's why each step also contains practical exercises for you to complete, as it's only through action rather than merely thinking about things that we can truly "rewire" the mind to do what we want it to do.

A short note: This book is written from the perspective of a heterosexual male and aimed primarily at men, but the scourge of a midlife crisis can, of course, strike at any gender or sexuality. If you're a woman who's stumbled upon the book and looking for some guidance, then don't worry — it'll still help. I refer to "women" "wives" and "girlfriends" throughout the book for ease of style, but it doesn't matter at all whether you're gay or straight. All that's required is your dedication to beating this thing. So, enough of the small print, let's get to it.

STEP ONE

YES, I AM OVER THIRTY-FIVE

"I'm a person who gets better with practice. Getting older is awesome because you get more practice."
– Zooey Deschanel

The other day an email from a major cinema chain dropped uninvited into my inbox. Usually I'd have just clicked delete and moved on, but being a movie fan I decided to give it a read. It turned out they were promoting a special discount for movie-goers aged fifty-five and over, called "Silver Cinema". As well as a patronizing title, the offer also included fifteen percent off any afternoon movie, plus complimentary tea and biscuits. In Britain today, it seems, to be over fifty-five means you have gray hair, enjoy "aromatic tea, coffee and buttery biscuits" and have nothing better to do in the middle of the afternoon than sit around watching movies.

It's moments like these that make me realize not only how condescending people in their teens, twenties and early thirties are when it comes to anyone older than them, but also how obsessed we've become with age in general. An obsession which I believe is one of the root causes of men's midlife crises.

Let's take a look at a few basic truths:

- Every single person on this planet, every second of every day, is getting older.
- Everyone will be the same age as everyone else at some point in time.
- There is always someone younger than you, and always someone older.

I admit that these are hardly the most groundbreaking nuggets of information you're ever likely to have digested, but I repeat them here as they appear to have quietly been forgotten by a startlingly large proportion of the human race.

I can't speak for all countries but in the West, in general, and certainly in the wonderfully sunny and vibrant island I'm from, we've become obsessed with age. Open up a newspaper and you're sure to be informed exactly how old everyone is, whether it's relevant to the story or not. Turn on the TV and you'll be told exactly how old each contestant is in a game show. People are always asking how old you are, even if you tell them once a year.

According to a recent study, the British think youth officially ends at age thirty-five and old age starts at fifty-nine — in other words, you're considered an old man six years *before* you retire. It may come as no surprise to learn then that Britain came top in a list of countries considered the most ageist in Europe. The Greeks, on the other hand, stipulate that old age starts at sixty-eight, so it really does depend on where you live with these things.

As soon as we pass the age of around twenty-four, it seems we can be labeled as "old" for no other reason than the person you're talking to happens to be younger. Since passing this magic number many years ago, I've constantly had people (often who I've only just met) ask me how old I am. And often being shocked or horrified when I tell them. I remember being on a date with a twenty-six year old girl, and when I told her I was thirty-four she got up and fled out the bar. When I was thirty-three, a guy at work found out my age and called me an "old man". He was twenty-seven. I can also recall being twenty-four and telling a new work colleague how old I was and he winced — a sharp intake of breath followed by an "oh dear" rueful shake of the head. I have no idea how old he was. Probably twenty-three.

The problem is this: we've become defined to a large extent by how we old are and what that means in relation to our current position in life. In other words, it's a way of judging people. When someone asks how old you are, very often what they really want to know is where you are in life, and then judge you accordingly. If you're working in a record store and you're twenty-one, that's fine. But if you're working in a record store and you're thirty-one, well, eyebrows will be raised.

Overall, there's a systematic cultural brainwashing going on in many (particularly Western) societies that stipulate young equals beautiful, vibrant, healthy and appealing, while old equals ugly, sterile, diseased and repulsive. In many areas of life, from healthcare to employment, you're pretty much viewed as a washed-up burden on society once you hit sixty. In Hollywood, aging is either seen as something comical or sad, but generally best avoided, and the chances are all of this is having some sort of causal affect on your midlife crisis. Fine, you might say. But what the heck am I supposed to do about it?

STOP PLAYING ALONG

Let's imagine for a moment a world without age. Imagine a world in which everyone knows the date they were born, but nobody cares when it was or bothers to celebrate it. A world in which nobody labels anyone else with an "age" in the sense we do now. There are no "teenagers" "middle aged people" or "senior citizens", and people look at you like you're crazy if you ask how old they are.

Now think about how much better you'd feel.

Think about how great it'd be to just be you, and without the baggage of You + Your Age. No more panicking over upcoming birthdays. No more having to state your age on all those pesky forms. No more embarrassment at dating someone younger or older than yourself. In this world, age is only an issue when it needs to be. For example when you need to vote, take a driving test or gain entry into a nightclub. Personally, I know I'd feel much better about my age if society didn't make such a big deal over it, while also placing such an emphasis on youth. If no one cared how old anyone else was, and didn't worship the fresh complexions and lithe bodies of the young, we'd all be left to behave as we feel rather than going through life constantly worrying about what age number we happen to be at any given moment.

If you're suffering from a midlife crisis, the chances are you're unhappy about your age. But would you be as unhappy if you lived in a society like the one described above? Before my own midlife crisis I used to constantly fret about how old I was. In my forties I wished I was still in my thirties, in my thirties I wished I was still in my twenties, and in my twenties I wished I was still a teenager. This is called living in your head rather than in the present moment, and is no way to live. It's pointless worrying over the inevitable. However, once you begin to view age as just one big societal construct — one that you don't have to go along with if you don't want to — you should find some of your age-related anxiety begin to lift.

I guess you could say "age is just a number" too, but that's easy to dismiss as a trifling cliché. You need to really sit down and think about this on a deeper level. Do you really want to live your life in a constant state of anxiety over something that you absolutely can't control? Something that's happening to everyone? An illusory "age" that's only important because your society says it is? The fact is, the less attached you can become to societal constructs like age, money, ethnicity and religion, the happier you'll be. It's time to stop playing along with man-made ideas if they're bringing you down. You don't have to if you don't want to. Stop asking people how old they are and stop telling people how old you are when they ask. Whenever someone used to ask me how old I was, I used to sheepishly tell them. Now I just palm them off with "eighty-six" and move on.

Difficult as it may be, what you need to try to do is stop playing along with society's obsession with age. Try to keep these three points in mind when doing this:

Stop playing along. "Young" "middle-aged" and "old", are really just societal constructs. Don't judge yourself (or other people) based on illusory societal constructs.

Young people missed the good times. Make a list of all the things you're grateful you were around for that this generation's completely missed out on. Like decent music, for example. Or to be able to walk down the street without bumping into someone glued to their phone.

Take care of yourself. You're also much more likely to feel old if you're not taking as much care of your body as you should. If you've got a beer belly and can't sprint fifty yards without collapsing then it's no wonder you're feeling older than you should. It comes down to whether you want to do something about your health and fitness, or simply coast on feeling old. I go into this in more detail in Step Nine, but for now have a think about if you were in as good a shape as Tom Cruise (who's currently fifty-four and still beating people up on screen as Jack Reacher) whether you'd feel as old as you do.

* * *

DIG DEEPER

Learn How To Live Young, Think Young, Be Young… At Any Age – There aren't many out there but this is a great book on aging: https://www.bullpub.com/catalog/Live-Young-Think-Young-Be-Young

Dare To Question Why We Are So Afraid Of Getting Older – TED talk in which Scilla Elworthy discusses how to navigate agism: https://www.youtube.com/watch?v=J6zenOjPC1A

7 Real Strategies To Combat Ageism – Article by psychology professor, Susan Krauss Whitbourne: http://www.huffingtonpost.com/susan-krauss-whitbourne/combat-ageism_b_9720708.html

Older People Are Happier – You may be going through a midlife crisis now, but in this TED talk, Laura Carstensen talks about the benefits of aging: https://www.youtube.com/watch?v=7gkdzkVbuVA

24 people who became highly successful after reaching the age of 40 – Get inspired by those who show it's never too late: http://www.independent.co.uk/news/business/analysis-and-features/24-people-who-became-highly-successful-after-reaching-the-age-of-40-a6732216.html

STEP TWO

THE #1 CAUSE OF ALL YOUR PAIN

"Whenever I climb I am followed by a dog called Ego."
– Friedrich Nietzsche

What would you say is the number one cause for not only all your pain, but all the pain misery and suffering that exists in the world? No, it's not Adam Sandler's movies, it's the ego.

Every bad emotion, argument, fight and war in history can trace its origins back to that little voice inside our heads that gives us a sense of self. Contrary to common wisdom, the ego is not just an "inflated sense of self", it's your mind's *perception of self*, whether it happens to be inflated or not. By perception of self I mean anything that you strongly identify with and regard as "you". This could be anything from your name, to your favorite band or variety of frozen yoghurt. Anything with which you form a strong mental attachment becomes part of this sense of self and therefore your ego, or the part of your mind which says "this is me". Whenever you or someone else says "I hate musicals", or "I love wrestling", or "I'm a member of X political party and I support everything they say", that's the ego talking.

THE FIRST AIM OF THE EGO IS TO PROTECT YOU

All your ego really wants is to protect you from danger. It does this by making us react in different ways to different circumstances. Let's say you come home after work to find an intruder attacking your wife. Well it's your ego that pushes you into fight mode. But if you're out hiking in a forest and stumble upon a grizzly bear, then it kicks you into flight mode. On the other hand, when you're too scared to go and talk to a woman in a bar, that's your ego's "Whoa, there's no way I'm not doing that" response.

In fact, any situation that your ego regards as dangerous and as a potential threat to you (but really itself), will fire up one of these three responses.

As you can probably gather, this is all well and good when the ego's getting involved in real dangers to your personal well-being, such as cars out of control, bomb alerts and on-rushing bears. This is your ego doing its job to save your life at all costs, as instructed by thousands of years of evolutionary programming. Problems can arise, though, when the mind identifies a little too strongly with the ego and ends up listening to it when it shouldn't. Asking someone out, standing up to a boss, holding a speech in front of twenty people, are all imagined fears in which you won't actually come to any physical harm. And yet the ego still elicits a "Whoa, there's no way I'm not doing that" response which involves sweating, nerves, dribbling etc., in an effort to protect you (itself). Unfortunately, it's this response system that's holding you, and the majority of the human race, back.

THE SECOND AIM OF THE EGO IS TO ALWAYS BE RIGHT

The ego has a very black and white view of the world in which it loves to position itself as a victim up against a constant series of "enemies". These enemies could be anyone from a stranger in the street to your best friend, or from a political viewpoint to an entire country. The ego loves to attack or become defensive whenever it thinks it's being "wronged", and will always, *always*, think it's right. Hence the reason why people find it so hard to get along on this planet.

When it comes to your midlife crisis, it's important to remember that it's not really "you" that's causing your pain. It's your ego that's in the driving seat when you're gripped by fear, doubt, unhappiness, anger, judgment, insecurity and all the other wonderful emotions that go along with a midlife crisis. Now, this may all sound a little new agey if you're not familiar with it, but it's important to remember that your ego doesn't represent your "true self". Your ego is an illusion. Your true self is "consciousness" "awareness" or whatever you wish to call it, and embraces the present moment while your ego fears it.

In other words, you never *really* feel anxious, fearful, dissatisfied, or threatened. Your ego does. But it tricks you into believing it's you that's feeling that way. Keeping you in a constant state of anxiety, fear and unhappiness in your life is your ego's way of trying to protect you (itself) from threats that don't actually exist. By stopping you from standing up to your wife, starting your own business, or whatever else your ego deems too scary, in reality all it's doing is holding you back. Luckily, the ego isn't very good at standing up to scrutiny. Once you recognize it for what it is — an illusion that in trying to protect you actually does more harm than good — it shrinks in size and loses its power. Simply recognizing that it's your ego that's making you feel like your life is one big screw up, will immediately make it that much easier to combat.

In order to bring the ego under some sort of control and start regaining power over your life, I highly recommend this little technique called "watching the ego".

HOW TO "WATCH" YOUR EGO

Start by taking a moment to think about something that bothers or annoys you. It could be anything, just make sure it's something that's really gotten under your skin and that you can't get out of your head. A frustrating situation at work, maybe. Or an argument you had with a friend several months ago. Dwell on these feelings of regret, anxiety or anger for a moment. Think about all ways you've been mistreated and "wronged" by this person or situation. Consider all the "if only's" and what you should've said but didn't. Feeling pretty bad? Good.

Now I want you to have a go at merely noticing yourself as being full of regret, anxious or angry. Step back and simply observe these thoughts whirring away inside your mind. Once you've recognized them, become aware that these thoughts which position you as a victim up against an "oppressor", are coming from your ego. This may be difficult at first but just practice noticing whenever you become lost in negative thought patterns during the day, and try to realize each time that this is your ego talking and not necessarily "you". This is important because it forces you to see the difference between your ego generating negative thoughts and emotions, and who you really are which is "awareness" of your ego.

These angry, judgmental, fearful thoughts and emotions are your ego at work and have nothing whatsoever to do with who you truly are. How can they be if you're able to notice them? Once you begin to disassociate yourself from your thoughts in this way, you'll soon find that you're able to better control your ego and therefore your negative emotions about how bad your life is right now. The basis of this technique can be found in the practice of meditation which is the single best way to free yourself from the endless noise and "monkey chatter" in your head, and this is what I'll be discussing in Step Four.

Do this immediately: Go and order the book below by Eckhart Tolle — probably the best ever written on the ego and the nature of the self.

* * *

DIG DEEPER

How Your Ego Dictates Your Entire Life – Great video from Leo Gura on the ego:
https://www.youtube.com/watch?v=xqLlXz0k_qM

What Is Ego? – Life coach, Noah Hammond, tells you how to identify and bypass it: http://bit.ly/2g3pGJw

A New Earth – One of the best books on the ego ever written:
https://www.eckharttolle.com/books/newearth/

The Ego Illusion – Video featuring the voice of the godfather of Western spirituality, Alan Watts:
http://www.youtube.com/watch?v=xAdMbNl8u2M&list=PLC0oot YAmSwvniDO_aSuu_5S1vdZw4KvQ

The Ego In Plain Terms – Introductory video on the workings of the ego from Sean Webb: http://iamspirituality.com/i-am-spirituality-ep-0005-the-ego

STEP THREE

THE CURSE OF MONKEY CHATTER

"We are dying from overthinking. We are slowly killing ourselves by thinking about everything. Think. Think. Think. You can never trust the human mind anyway. It's a death trap."
– Anthony Hopkins

I'd like to kick off this step with a thought exercise that pretty much sums up the essence of a midlife crisis.

THE MAN ON THE BRIDGE

Imagine you're in San Francisco on a clear summer's day looking at the Golden Gate bridge through a pair of binoculars. As you scan the cars and people moving along this magnificent feat of engineering, you notice a young man standing alone. At first glance he appears normal — outwardly healthy, wearing a shirt and jeans — but as you linger on him a moment, you realize that he seems distressed. He's pacing up and down, looking over the railings and occasionally holding his head in his hands. It dawns on you that this guy might be considering jumping into the water 220 feet below.

Now pull back and observe everything else that's going on around the man once again: cars streaming by, tourists posing for pictures, a bright sun high up in a cloudless blue sky. In other words, notice how there's nothing wrong in his world outside of his own head. There's only the *present moment,* which is just another sunny day. As I said, this scenario perfectly sums up how thoughts and emotions can hijack reality, often to the point where we get dragged down into things like midlife crises, depression and suicidal tendencies. The man on the bridge has let negative thoughts about his past, and pessimism about his future, block out the fact that all that really matters is the present.

You can test this yourself by dwelling a moment on something you think is bringing your life down. It can be a situation from the past, in the present, or in the future. Now look around and take stock of your physical environment. What do you actually see, hear and feel? I presume you're not sitting in a burning building, running from a stampede of wildebeest, or in the midst of a having a stroke. If so, what *is* going on around you? My guess is nothing that's putting your life under any kind of actual physical threat, so take a moment to notice how everything's fine *outside of your own head*.

Breathe in the air. Take a look around. Listen to sounds. And let it sink in how everything in the present moment is always okay. You may have regrets about the past, worries about the future, or real problems in your life, but none of them can hurt you right now in this present moment. This is a useful exercise in remembering that it's usually our *response* to events that hurt us, not the actual events themselves.

JUST WHAT IS A MIDLIFE CRISIS ANYWAY?

When you break it down to its bare essentials, a midlife crisis can be seen as merely a collection of thoughts and emotions. Thoughts that exist only in your mind, and emotions that exist only in your body. For example, would you still consider yourself to be in the midst of a midlife crisis if you never dwelt on negative thoughts or had a negative emotional reaction to them? Isn't the only reason you're suffering from this condition because to some extent you're choosing to give a disproportionate amount of mind-space to it? Think about it: if you never allowed yourself to become embroiled in endless ruminations about the past, the future, and the state of your life in general, would you technically still suffer from a midlife crisis?

You might say, Okay, but I can't help agonizing over the past and the future. What do I do? This is true to a point. You can't control the random thoughts that pop in and out of your head, whether they're negative or not, but you can control whether you choose to dwell on these thoughts. You can choose to stop yourself from focusing on the bad hand life's supposedly dealt you while sitting on the bus, lying in bed at night, or wherever you are, if you wish. Granted this can be hard, but it's far from impossible.

I will go into how exactly you can do this in a later step. For now, let's take a look at both of these phenomena — thoughts and emotions — in a bit more detail.

THOUGHTS 101

Who comes to mind if I ask you to think of a famous movie star? Take a moment to see who pops in your head. Leonardo DiCaprio? Whoopie Goldberg? Ginger Rogers? Whoever it was, how did that *particular* person enter your mind? What process just happened that brought them from your subconscious to your conscious mind? The truth is, while we generally have no trouble picturing an image, recalling a memory, working out a problem, contemplating an idea, or remembering a tune at will, we're remarkably ignorant of what thoughts actually are and where they come from. Even neuroscientists remain pretty clueless about the precise nature of human consciousness, which should tell you something.

Here's what we do know: thoughts can dramatically affect your physical health. Positive ones make it better, and negative ones make it worse. Despite the fact that thoughts don't exist in any real sense of the word outside of our own heads — they're just neurons firing around the brain in a complex series of electrical and chemical reactions — they're responsible to a large extent for our personal well-being and happiness, or lack of it.

Negative thoughts are kind of the ground zero of your midlife crisis, as they lead onto negative emotions (and sometimes then on to negative actions). The funny thing is, these thoughts are almost certainly not even accurate. They're just made up stories your mind is telling itself over and over because, after years of repetition, it's simply fallen into the habit of doing so. The ego always wants to paint you as a victim in the past and always wants to assume the worst in the future, but this is just your mind playing tricks on you — forcing you to see things in a negative rather than positive light. However, once you start to notice what it's up to, these negative thoughts will begin to lose their so-called significance.

WHY THOUGHTS ARE REALLY JUST WEEDY LITTLE BRATS

When you wake up in the morning, is your head full of positive thoughts? Are you happy that a new day has begun, full of love for your family and friends and so leap out of bed excited to get started? Or, upon waking up, does your mind immediately turn to negative, grouchy thoughts about wasted years and opportunities? Or anger over something that happened weeks, months or years ago?

Much like how the nightly news focuses on violent distressing stories over peaceful happy ones, so our minds love to focus on the depressing stories we tell ourselves about our own lives. Your mind/ego can't be bothered to dwell on the good things that may be happening in your own life. It doesn't really care how great your wife or job is, or the fact you rescued someone from drowning last week. It's more concerned with keeping you preoccupied with threats to your well-being, whether real or imaginary, and painting you as a victim rather than a hero.

Let's get right down to brass tacks: thoughts are a pain in the neck. Well, not all thoughts, but the whiny repetitive ones we let drown out the positive life-affirming ones. The ones we let crowd our minds and jump up and down vying for our attention. At the moment you're letting them succeed, but that's what this book will help you put a stop to.

EMOTIONS 101

Negative emotions are simply our bodily reactions to these negative thoughts. If you reflected on your past positively, for example, you wouldn't have negative emotions about it in the present.

Sean Webb, founder of the *I Am Spirituality* website, has developed an easily understood, scientifically peer-reviewed equation which explains how emotions work within each and every one of us. It goes like this:

$$(EP - RP = ER)$$

Expectation or Preference – Reality as Perceived

= Emotional Response

In a nutshell, this means our Expectation or Preference is how we would like, or expect, something we're emotionally attached to, to be or turn out. Our Reality as Perceived is then how something actually is, or what actually happens. And finally, our Emotional Response is conditioned by this Reality as Perceived. In other words, if our Reality as Perceived meets our Expectation or Preference, we experience a positive emotion. If it falls below our Expectation or Preference, then we experience a negative emotion.

Here's a brief analysis of how your emotions are working when applied to your midlife crisis. Let's say your Emotional Preference is that you spent your twenties and thirties as a professional tennis player, winning two major championships a year and hanging out in-between with Maria Sharapova on a yacht. Your Reality as Perceived, however, is that an injury ruined your career just as it was getting started and you wound up a sports teacher at your local college. Therefore, you experience a negative Emotional Response.

This frustration at things not turning out as you planned also applies to other people who you're emotionally attached to. For example, you discover one day that when your girlfriend was single she used to sometimes enjoy having sex with two guys at once, which may cause a negative Emotional Response. As I mentioned in the section on the ego, anything which falls within its sense of self — you, your partner, your favorite movie, etc. — can all be affected by these emotional responses.

THE VICIOUS CIRCLE

Thoughts and emotions about the past and the future are inextricably linked, but there is a specific process that's occurring every time you let negative thoughts and emotions put you in a bad mood. This exercise will help you back away from this downward spiral of thoughts and emotions and, over time, break the so-called power they have over you.

Let's start by taking a look at what this downward spiral entails:

1. A negative thought is triggered by something, or pops involuntarily in the mind
2. A negative emotion arises in the body
3. A cycle of negative thoughts and emotions begins

The gap between each stage may be a micro-second, but it's impossible to feel upset, tormented, angry, anxious or any emotion at all without first thinking about it. All emotions can be physically felt in the body — usually in the chest or stomach — and from here it's all too easy to spiral down into a vicious circle of overthinking and overreacting.

Have a think again about a few of the problems you believe are causing of your midlife crisis. Let your mind drift into its usual negative thought patterns, for example surrounding a boring job, a sense of pointlessness or a major regret. Having dwelt on these thoughts for a moment, begin to notice how they make you feel. What emotions are you experiencing? And where are you feeling them? In your head, chest or stomach? From here you would usually get dragged into a vicious circle of overthinking, but now you're going to take a step back and just notice them. Feel how they're just self-inflicted thoughts and emotions confined to your own mind and body, while your outer reality is actually no threat at all.

Here's the three-step process you should follow to help quell this vicious circle of thoughts and emotions inside you:

1. Become aware of the thoughts and emotions. You can't prevent these negative thoughts and emotions from popping up in your brain and body, but you can control how you choose to react to them. When thoughts and emotions like these arise, simply notice them.

2. Take a step back. Disassociate yourself from your own thoughts and emotions by recognizing them as merely neurons and sensations, and without judgment or resistance. Doing this removes you from your anxious state and grounds you once again in the present moment. It creates a gap in which your mind is able to recognize the difference between what's real — the right here and now — and what's not — the stories your mind is making up.

3. Focus on something else. Do whatever it takes to prevent yourself from slipping down into a wormhole of overthinking. Read a book. Call a friend. Dance around the room naked to your favorite song. Whatever it is, stop thinking and start doing. Break the cycle enough times like this and your mind will begin to find it easier to do by itself.

I'm not saying any of this is easy, but as Beverly Sills once said, "There are no shortcuts to any place worth going". And once you've mastered it, you'll feel like nothing can touch you. Over time you should begin to feel less and less of an emotional reaction every time you have a negative thought, and finally they'll just pop in and out of your mind like any other inconsequential thought.

* * *

DIG DEEPER

Think And Grow Rich – Seminal book by Napoleon Hill on the power of thought: http://www.naphill.org/shop/books/think-and-grow-rich/

The Science Of Emotions – TED talk by Jaak Panksepp: https://www.youtube.com/watch?v=65e2qScV_K8

How Do We Break Excessive Thinking? – Clip from an Eckhart Tolle Q&A: http://www.youtube.com/watch?v=dTFDfR47dl4

The Equation Of Emotion – Video from Sean Webb on the equation of emotion: http://www.youtube.com/watch?v=6-60Mwkbt8c

Getting Stuck In The Negatives – Professor Alison Ledgerwood TED talk on how to get unstuck: https://www.youtube.com/watch?v=7XFLTDQ4JMk

STEP FOUR

...AND YOUR ASS WILL FOLLOW

"Empty your mind. Be formless, shapeless, like water."
– Bruce Lee

I was never one for anything remotely new-agey like yoga, astrology or dancing around in a white robe while "high on love", but I have to say I found learning how to meditate to be probably the most beneficial skill I learnt in controlling my midlife crisis. This is because meditation is the means by which we are able to fully realize the experience of being fully in the now, and simply observe our thoughts and emotions rather than being overwhelmed by them. Through meditation, we're able to better tap into the fact that the past and the future don't exist and that nothing can hurt us in the present moment. Certainly not mere thoughts or emotions.

Regular mediation has been scientifically proven to reduce the stress generated by the brain. You may be surprised to learn that when we get anxious and stressed about things a part of our brains literally becomes "enflamed". The part that becomes enflamed is an almond shaped set of neurons located in the temporal lobe, known as the amygdala. This is where the emotion of fear is located and where defense responses are mobilized when it thinks we're in danger — the advancing man with a knife, the plane out of control, the relationship that's going "too well", etc.

When we become flooded with negative and stressful thoughts, the amygdala releases a whole host of chemicals such as adrenaline and cortisol which increase heart rate, blood pressure and literally damage the brain without us even realizing it. Just by thinking certain thoughts, choosing to perceive them the way you do and constantly dwelling on them, your brain and body are suffering by having to repeatedly activate their stress mechanisms.

In fact, what you need to be doing is the complete opposite, i.e. replace these stress responses with relaxation responses. All of which also reduces the chances of getting certain diseases, as well as improves cognitive functioning and a whole host of other benefits.

Therefore, if you're not already meditating, now might be a good time to start as it trains the mind to stop racing backwards and forwards in time and remain at peace in the present. The type of mediation I recommend is called mindfulness, but you can choose whichever kind you like. In the Dig Deeper section at the end of this step you'll find plenty of options.

HOW TO PRACTICE MINDFULNESS IN 3 EASY STEPS

Find a quiet place to sit or lie down. Make sure you're alone and won't be disturbed. Then, set an alarm to go off in ten or twenty minutes, and then follow these three steps. (Leave your eyes open or closed, whichever you prefer.)

1. Breathe. Take five deep breaths and relax every muscle in your body.

2. Become aware. Simply become aware of what's happening around and within you, moment-by-moment and non-judgmentally. Focus on the present moment. The here and now. Concentrate on your breathing, or how your body feels in the chair. Listen to sounds in the room. Look at the patterns on the wallpaper. Alternate between all of these things if you wish, but the most important thing is to just observe whatever's happening, as it happens. When a thought appears in the mind, simply observe this too, just as you would an external event.

3. Acknowledge and start again. As you observe your thoughts and the world around you, you may find your mind has drifted away and become lost in thought. Whenever this happens, just acknowledge that it's happened (without judgment) and return your attention to the present moment — your breathing, the sounds outside, images in your mind, a breeze in your hair or whatever it is you notice. That's all meditation is — the continual process of pulling your mind back from being lost in thought to the present moment.

That's all there is to it. I found twenty-ish minutes meditation a day worked best for me, but some people like to do it for just five minutes, and some for half an hour. I suggest starting with five minutes and then working your way up to fifteen, twenty or as many as you like. You can choose any of the mediation methods out there but if you've never practiced it before I highly recommend starting with a guided meditation — i.e. listening to someone talk you through it on a pre-recorded track. Sam Harris's guided mediation included in the Dig Deeper section is really great, and I found listening to the twenty-five minute version every day worked perfectly for me when I was starting out.

Now, I remember trying to meditate in the past and it didn't seem to work. It felt like I was just staring at a wall and nothing happened. If you experience this, that's okay, but I found what really helped was discovering that when you do these deep meditative exercises, you are literally triggering a relaxation nerve in your brain called the vagus nerve. This nerve runs from your brain, via the heart and lungs, all the way down to the abdomen. When it's stimulated through deep breathing and meditation, the amygdala calms down and the fire is put out. Do this regularly enough and it will help the amygdala stop flaring up in the first place.

Much of the stress we experience in life is simply caused by overthinking which triggers a reaction in the amygdala, and when I realized that I was fighting this by stimulating a nerve, I took the whole process more seriously and was able to reap the benefits. However, it's common for new practitioners of meditation to keep it up for a couple of weeks and then drop it when it starts to become boring or feel like a waste of time.
While this is perfectly understandable it's also a mistake, as the effects of meditation are usually only felt after around six weeks — the time it takes for the brain to build new neural pathways. It's then that you should start to feel generally calmer during day to day life and really begin to better be able to control your thoughts and emotions.

THE EGO VS. YOUR TRUE SELF

I've mentioned a few times so far the concept of the ego being responsible for negative thoughts rather than your true self.

Well, meditation is the key to beginning to see this more clearly. By making you more aware of the present moment, meditation forces you to become more attuned to your true self by getting in touch with that part of you that simply observes experience (including thought) as it happens, rather than analyze it, critique it and judge it through the lens of the ego.

A good analogy to explain this is to equate our thoughts as cars whizzing by on a busy street. Imagine each car is a thought that comes and goes. It appears and disappears as quickly as it arrived. Now imagine that you're standing in the middle of the street and the cars (thoughts) are whizzing by in both directions. Then, begin floating up above the street so you're now looking down on the cars as they come and go. This is akin to meditating and being in the state of your true self. You are now looking down and observing your thoughts, but you're not down on the ground experiencing them. You're simply watching them go by.

The ego tricks you into believing that *you are* your thoughts and emotions and that you identify with them, but meditation opens up the reality that you are not your thoughts or emotions. If you're witnessing a thought or emotion, then how can it be "you"? You are, in fact, the "awareness" that's doing the witnessing.

ALL WE HAVE IS NOW

John Lennon once said "Life happens when you're busy making other plans", and this is the essence of our problem with time. We're always looking backwards to the past or forwards to the future without ever just enjoying what we have now, in the present. Much of the anxiety generated during a midlife crisis is caused by this strange phenomena of always wanting something other than what you have.

Rather than living in the now and enjoying life for what it is, you're maybe tending to wish you were somewhere else and that things had been different in the past so you could be somewhere else now in the present. And this causes you to constantly plan ahead for the future when finally "things will work out" and you'll be happy. But how do you know you'll be happy once you've got there? And how will you know you're there in the first place? Unless you change the way you think and let yourself sink into the present, you'll always be looking back and ahead, wishing things could be different. But the only answer is to learn to live in the now.

When you're thinking about the past or the future and feeling nauseous about them, it's important to remember that you're actually thinking about stories created in the mind, rather than something that actually exists anywhere outside of your own head. This is because, if we look at life as a series of experiences, moment by moment, both the past and the future are illusions. The past has already been and gone and the future is yet to arrive, and so what are you left with? The right here and now — this present moment, reading these words on a screen.

This may seem an obvious point to make, but is it possible to do anything outside of the now? Are you able to make a single action or think a single thought that happens in the past or the future? No. But when suffering from a midlife crisis this fundamental truth seems to somehow slip by the wayside. Instead, you may hate the past and fear the future, despite the fact that neither of them exist in any meaningful sense. There is absolutely nothing you can do about the past or the future, and so to worry about either has to be one of the biggest wastes of time and energy the mind could come up with. But then that's the ego for you.

It can be helpful to think of ourselves as having an Existing Self and a Remembering Self. Our Existing Self is, of course, how we experience life — moving from moment to moment, day to day and year to year. Our Remembering Self is what constitutes our memories and is the part of ourselves that no longer exists. We're only able to do anything from the stand point of the Existing Self. Hence, even if we're thinking about the past in our Remembering Self, it's through the perspective of the Existing Self.

Your past experiences, therefore, are part of your Remembering Self, but you can only access them through your Existing Self, which is in the present. So, starting today, try to focus your mind on these truths and you should find it hard to feel negatively about your past or future when you begin to see them for what they are: illusions.

* * *

DIG DEEPER

Meditation, A Beginner's Practical Guide – Video tutorial on the many benefits of meditation from dating coach, Owen Cook: http://bit.ly/2gKXhw5

The Best Meditation Apps – List of meditation apps for your smartphone: https://www.outsideonline.com/1926181/best-meditation-apps

The Mirror Of Mindfulness – Audio guided meditation from Sam Harris: http://www.samharris.org/blog/item/mindfulness-meditation

Why Meditate? – Enlightening interview with major meditation teacher, Joseph Goldstein: https://www.samharris.org/podcast/item/why-meditate

Why Meditation Is Critical And The Types You Can Try – Great introductory video on various meditation techniques from Sean Webb: http://www.blubrry.com/iamspirituality/1776586/i-am-0096-why-meditation-is-critical-and-the-types-you-can-try

STEP FIVE

YOU ALREADY HAVE IT ALL

"Nowadays people know the price of everything and the value of nothing."
– Oscar Wilde

There's a scene in one of my favorite movies, *Annie Hall*, in which Alvy explains his view of life to Annie:

"I feel that life is divided up into the horrible and the miserable, those are the two categories, y'know? The horrible would be like, I don't know, terminal cases like blind people, crippled… I don't know how they get through life, it's amazing to me. And the miserable is everyone else. So, when you go through life you should be thankful that you're miserable."

As Alvy says, maybe it's time to start being thankful that you're just miserable. Maybe it's not going quite the way you planned, but do want to know how good your life is compared to the majority of the human race that's now living, *or has ever lived,* on this planet?

THINGS COULD ALWAYS BE WORSE

Have you heard of a guy called Nick Vujicic? He's a Serbian-Australian motivational speaker (and Christian evangelist, but nobody's perfect) who was born with Phocomelia — a rare disorder that causes severe birth defects, especially of the upper limbs. In Nick's case, this resulted in him being born with no arms and no legs. He's also happily married, successful and has a kid. Imagine you'd been born with no arms and no legs. Or with one of the many other birth defects out there, such as dwarfism (failure to grow to normal size), ambras syndrome (excessive facial and body hair), progeria (excessive aging), and so on.

Imagine you'd been born, or had found yourself, in any one of the hundreds of "horrible" categories out there: blind, deaf, dumb, terminally ill, and so on. Or that you were born in the midst of a war zone, say in Africa or the Middle East, and every day's a struggle just to stay alive. Or that you've been convicted of a crime you didn't commit and sentenced to death. You wouldn't have the time or the head space to suffer from a midlife crisis.

In 2016 there was much talk that it was "the worst year ever". This means it was worse than being hit by a plague outburst in the fourteenth century. Or living in an East End slum in 1880s London. Or being lined up and shot during Lenin, Hitler or Mao's purges. However, the list of genuinely worst circumstances you *could have* experienced due to sheer bad luck is endless. But right now you're living in the best time there's ever been to be alive. A time that billions upon billions of people now dead never had the chance to experience. *But you do.* Whenever you sometimes feel like your life is crappy, monotonous or pointless, take a moment to remind yourself that there are a million ways it could be worse. Much worse. Maybe your life isn't as bad as you think it is.

WHAT ARE THE ODDS?

13.7 billion years ago. A hot dense mass about the size of pea, bursts. The resulting colossal explosion of energy flings matter at an incomprehensible speed in all directions, billions of mile wide, creating the universe as we now know it. As the universe expands, energy cools and matter congeals into atoms. Gravity crushes them together causing them to ignite and form our solar system.

4.5 billion years ago. Clouds of dust, rocks and ice orbiting the newly formed sun, get pulled together by the force of gravity into one giant clump, forming Earth. Then, another planet smashes into Earth and the resulting debris clusters again under the force of gravity, forming the moon. This collision also tips the Earth onto its axis, giving us our four seasons. Microbial life — a kind of bacterium — appears in Earth's seas soon afterwards.

2.5 billion years ago. Photosynthesis is born when some microbial life forms living in the sea begin converting carbon dioxide in the air into food, using energy from the sun. This transforms Earth forever as oxygen gets pumped into the air — so much so that the sky turns from red to blue — and life explodes in complexity and variety as they harness the energy-giving properties in an oxygen rich atmosphere.

400 million years ago. Plant life and fungi successfully transition onto land.

250 — 220 million years ago. The Earth's landmasses converge to form one supercontinent. Mountains form when continents collide and earthquakes rip them apart. These teutonic shifts produce major climate changes, with the Earth tipping from very hot to very cold. Dinosaurs prove to be the most successful creatures to have ever existed, due to their ability to lay eggs inland and far from the sea. However, they are wiped out when a six mile wide asteroid slams into the Earth. Some mammals survive by taking to the water again and adapting back into life in the sea.

30 million years ago. Mammals migrate across the globe. Primates in Africa migrate to South America and eventually cross to Asia where they lose their tails, becoming apes.

3 million — 13,000 years ago. The first upright apes appear on the grassy plains of Africa and, roughly 1 million years later, begin using stone tools. Over the next 2 million years the brain size of humans increases substantially, probably due to increased hand-eye coordination, and they harness fire. Five-hundred-thousand years ago, neanderthals emerge, only to possibly be hunted to extinction by modern humans. Fifty-thousand years ago modern humans emerge in Africa, migrate across Europe and Asia reaching Australia about 40,000 years ago and the Americas about 13,000 years ago. Somewhere among these tribes of early humans, battling to survive against all the odds, are your direct descendants. And so begins another stage in the billions of events that led directly to you being born…

Apologies for the history lesson, but given these remarkable series of events what do you think were the odds that you'd actually be born? Turns out it's quite a big number — roughly one in 400 TRILLION. That's basically an unfathomable number of events that had to occur — from the Big Bang itself, to Earth being formed, to homo sapiens emerging victorious over every other species of human, to your parents meeting in a disco in 1968 — in order for you to actually arrive in this world. Think about this for a moment. It's INCREDIBLE.

I realize, of course, that it's not always useful to put the cart before the horse in these situations. If you were to throw a can of paint at a large canvas hanging on a wall, the chances of the paint landing exactly where it did is probably also one in 400 trillion. There were no odds involved — the paint just happened to land where it did. And the same is true of your chances of being born. You're not here on this planet because of chance and odds, but because a random, yet causal chain of events has happened, resulting in you being here. There's only one of you that's ever walked this Earth and there's only ever going to be one of you after you've gone, and that's pretty amazing.

AND YET YOU'RE MISERABLE?

Does your life feel purposeless? Are you drifting in a sea of ennui? Are you unable to drink more than three pints of beer anymore without getting a hangover? Maybe on the surface of things there's much to be disgruntled about. But stepping back every so often to have a think about how lucky you actually are to be here in the first place should help you start to see life a little differently. Believe me, I know how easy it is to always feel put upon and like life's somehow working against you. But it's not. It's just your perception that's making it seem like it is. In reality, your life is amazing simply due to the fact you're here is amazing. Remind yourself of this whenever life seems to be working against you, and take a moment to marvel at just how lucky you are.

There's a scene near the end of the movie *High Fidelity*, in which disgruntled record store owner, Rob (John Cusack), comes home to find his girlfriend, Laura, reading his list of top five dream jobs:

Rob: Hi, Laura.

Laura: (reading) "Top five dream jobs…"

Rob: Hey, that's private.

Laura: "Number one: journalist for *Rolling Stone* magazine, 1976 to 1979. Get to meet *The Clash*, Chrissie Hynde, *The Sex Pistols*, David Byrne. Get tons of free records. Number two: producer for *Atlantic Records*, 1964 to 1971. Get to meet Aretha, Wilson Pickett, Solomon Burke. More free records and a shit load of money. Number three: Any kind of musician — "

Rob: — besides classical or rap.

Laura: "I'd settle for being one of the *Memphis Horns* or something. I'm not asking to be Jagger, or Hendrix, or Otis Redding."

Rob: Uh-huh.

Laura: "Number four: film director."

Rob: Any except German or silent.

Laura: And number five… you have architect…

Rob: Yeah.

Laura: Seven years training…

Rob: I'm not sure I even wanna be an architect.

Laura: So you've got a list here of five things you'd do if qualifications, and time and history and salary were no object?

Rob: Yeah…

Laura: One of them you don't really wanna do anyway?

Rob: Well I did put it at number five.

Laura: Wouldn't you rather own your own record store than be an architect?

Rob: Yeah, I suppose.

Laura: And you wouldn't want to be a sixteenth century explorer, or the king of France…

Rob: God, no.

Laura: (writes) There you go then, dream job number five: <u>record store owner</u>.

Have a go at reframing your perception of what you already have. Maybe you're already living your dream and don't even realize it.

HOW MANY DAYS DO YOU HAVE LEFT?

In the winter of 2013, Wilko Johnson, guitarist with British dad rock band, *Dr Feelgood*, was diagnosed with terminal cancer. He was given under a year left to live. Luckily for him it turned out the doctors were wrong and his condition wasn't terminal, but treatable. "I suddenly felt intensely alive", he remembers. "Everything around me looked sharp and vibrant. I felt free. Free from the future and the past, free from everything but this present moment I was in". In other words, he finally truly valued the time he had on Earth.

I know I've mentioned that in essence, time is an illusion — there is no past or future, only the now — but the truth is you only have a finite amount of days left to enjoy being alive. Although comparing life expectancies across countries can be problematic, the average lifespan for men in the developed world is around seventy-six to eighty years old. That leaves you with how many years? Exactly. In fifty years time you very well might no longer be here. In a hundred years time you definitely won't be here. Depressing as that may be, it's also an opportunity to open up to life in the now — in this present moment — and to stop taking time for granted.

Let's imagine for a moment that you're forty-five. Let's then imagine you live until you're eighty-five. That means you have forty years left. If there are 365 days in a year, that means you have 14,600 days left. And if there are twenty-four hours in a day, that means you have 350,400 hours left. Which means that every hour that goes by is another one out of 350,400 that's lost forever, never to be recaptured. While this can be quite a depressing thought — a thought you maybe spend most of the time trying to avoid — it can also be quite a liberating one. Don't make the mistake of waiting until you're diagnosed with terminal cancer to come out the other side vowing never to take another day of their life for granted. Start now.

Start viewing time as a precious commodity and something that you'll never get back. Forget the old adage of living every day as if it's your last" because that's just impractical. What's not so impractical, though, is living each day while being more mindful of the present moment and how you use it.

It's time to take back your time and stop doing things you don't really want to do just to please other people. Stop watching movies or reading books just because you've started them. Stop spending hours watching drivel on TV. Stop taking your time left on this Earth for granted, because your life — this very moment — is slipping through your fingers. Now, you can either be terrified by this truth, or you can do something about it.

Here's another simple exercise you can start doing every day. Simply say to yourself as often as possible: I'm enjoying myself. No matter what you're doing, where you are, or how good or bad your day's actually going, just tell yourself that you're having a blast and watch how it immediately makes the world seem a better place. Try it the next time you're trying to flag down a cab in the rain, or stuck in an elevator with an obnoxious bore. You may be surprised.

* * *

DIG DEEPER

How To Stop Screwing Yourself Over – TED talk from Mel Robbins: https://www.youtube.com/watch?v=Lp7E973zozc

From The Beginning Of Time To The Present Day – Documentary on how we all got here: https://www.youtube.com/watch?v=_w-4OyYS2uE

Want to be happy? Be grateful – TED talk from David Steindl-Rast: https://www.youtube.com/watch?v=UtBsl3j0YRQ

Overcoming Hopelessness – TED talk from Nick Vujicic: https://www.youtube.com/watch?v=6P2nPI6CTlc

Human Evolution – A crash course fifteen minute video on the evolution of our species: https://www.youtube.com/watch?v=UPggkvB9_dc

STEP SIX

PAST ACTIONS, PRESENT TURMOIL

"I don't talk about the past."
– Prince

I have a friend named Marvin who was once a gifted footballer, or soccer player to our American readers. So gifted in fact, that at aged fourteen he was invited for a trial at a professional team. The date for the trial was set: eight a.m. on a Saturday morning. However, this was a tad too early for Marvin and so, rather than go along, he opted to stay in bed. He's been working at the same desk job for the past twenty years and regretted that Saturday morning ever since.

I have another friend named Rebecca who, while studying architecture at university, won a writing contest: an all expenses paid trip to Los Angeles to write for a TV show. The trouble was, this would mean skipping an important upcoming architecture exam. She decided not to take up the offer from the contest to go to LA. Instead, she became an architect, hated it, quit after ten years and is now currently unemployed. Now in their forties, both Rebecca and Marvin are less than thrilled with their lives and deeply regret their choices made in the past. "What if I'd gotten off my ass and gone to the trial?" Marvin complains. "Where would I be now if I'd moved to LA and written for that TV show?" Rebecca whines.

I too used to constantly fall victim to these kinds of regrets over choices made in my younger days. My mind used to be full of endless monkey chatter going over and over the same scenarios and missed opportunities like a broken record. "Why didn't I ask her out?" "Why did I waste so many years bumming around from job to job?" "Why didn't I travel more?" And on and on and on…

Just like Rebecca, Marvin and probably ninety percent of the population, I used to beat myself up over what an idiot I'd been on an almost daily basis. For some reason when it comes to regret and wishing we had behaved differently in the past, the biggest critic *by far* is ourselves. No one else churns over what we did in the past, or holds us accountable in quite the same unrelenting way as ourselves. The truth is, the only person who's probably giving you a hard time over all this, is you.

Very often we don't immediately regret the decisions we make. It's only after mulling over the problem in our heads, or when circumstances change, days, weeks or months after the event, that we re-label it in our minds as a bad choice and proceed to give ourselves an extraordinarily hard time over it. This, however, is pure madness if you consider that every action or non-action you regret in the past, was exactly what you wanted at that moment in time. Nobody was holding a gun to your head, forcing you to make that particular choice. You only made it because you alone wanted to make it, and for this reason it can be considered a true choice. By this I mean it was not only a choice that reflected what you truly wanted at that particular moment in time, but also who you were at that moment in time.

You may regret not backpacking across Europe, or starting your own company, or whatever it is, but it's time to reframe these past events in a positive rather than a negative light. You can try this by remembering what's good in your life right now and imagining what might've been if you'd taken the path all those years ago you now regret not taking. Is there something you'd potentially not have in your life now if you'd made a different decision in the past? Would you have, say, met your wife and had two wonderful kids if you'd decided to live in Australia for a year? And can you be sure that you would even be here? Maybe a car crash would've left you paralyzed, or worse. You just don't know. But you *do know* that you're here right now.

Two classic regrets for men, are often:

- **Career regrets**. This usually involves regretting not pursuing something more creative or life-fulfilling, such as being a musician, but also applies to more traditional work and career regrets too.

- **Romantic/sexual regrets**. These come in a variety of forms too. "The one that got away"— missing out on that one girl who slipped through your fingers — is a classic. As is generally regretting missed experiences: having more girlfriends or sleeping with more women before settling down.

However, some guys let these and other "bad" decisions haunt them for the rest of their lives, while others reframe them in their mind as learning opportunities and a necessary part of life. Given the chance, you may make a different choice today than in the past, but that's only because you've learnt from past mistakes. Today you're not the same person you were back then, so what else is there left to do but embrace the fact that there's nothing you could have done about it back then, even if you wanted to. And there's certainly nothing you can do about it now, so it's up to you whether you want to keep punishing yourself or let it go.

THE GRAND ILLUSION

We all have free will, right? Or do we? While it may feel like we're all free to think and do whatever we choose at any given moment, just how true is this? Are all of our choices in life completely within our control? Just how much free will do we really have? Without getting too deep into neuroscientific theory, the majority of scientists now believe that our sense of free will is in fact an illusion. Sam Harris, a philosopher and neuroscientist, puts it like this:

"The fact that our choices depend on prior cause does not mean that choice doesn't matter. To sit back and see what happens is also a choice that has its own consequences. So, the choices we make in life are as important as people think, but the next choice you make will come out of a wilderness of prior causes that you cannot see and did not bring into being."

In other words, the feeling that we're controlling our thoughts and actions is merely an illusion. We may think we're in control of them but in reality we're not. It's a myth. You may feel like you're making a conscious decision when you decide to buy a particular album, or date a particular person, or select sweet over salted popcorn at the movies, but most scientists would now agree that you're not. It has been scientifically proven that every so-called decision we make — from who to marry, to which pizza topping to go for — are not really arrived at by "us" but via a whole host of brain activities that we're not even aware of. (I'm no scientist, so please check out the videos and websites in the Dig Deeper section for a more robust explanation of "brain activities.")

If our thoughts precede our actions, then we should have free will in order to manipulate our actions by choosing our thoughts. But we don't. Instead, we're unable to choose which thoughts pop into our heads. An example of this is the "think of a movie star" question I asked in Step Three, but let's picture a president of the United States this time. Who pops into your consciousness? How and why did you think of them and not Richard Nixon? Did you "choose" for them to appear, or did they just appear like magic out of your subconscious? Therefore, if we're not the author of our thoughts, how can we really in any sense regard ourselves as having free will?

This applies not only to small choices but larger ones too — to things like why you prefer certain foods, clothes, or TV programs over others, and to why you're attracted to certain people over others. For example, I love Thomas Hardy novels and yet can't stand Jane Austen. Am I *choosing* to feel this way? Or is there just something within me that means I can read *Tess of the D'Urbervilles* fifteen times and yet can't get past the first chapter of *Pride and Prejudice* without slipping into a coma? I didn't choose this aspect of my personal tastes, it just "is". And the same applies to you.

FREE WILL AND LETTING GO OF REGRET

The knowledge that we don't have free will can help tremendously when it comes to overcoming regret. To regret often means to judge our own behavior and feel that we should or shouldn't have done certain things in the past. But if you didn't have free will, then you didn't really have the freedom to have done any differently.

If we're all just acting on the whim of our genes and neurons, why do we beat ourselves up so much over our past decisions? Whatever you regret was based on a variety of factors — your brain, your genes, your age, your life experience, your knowledge, your feeling on that particular day and so on. Given these factors, it's nonsensical to now regret that you didn't somehow make a different choice. How could you have done when your brain didn't give you the choice?

A great way of further neutralizing the pain of regrets is to make a Regrets List. Simply list all your regrets that still haunt you to this day. They can be major ones about the screw up of a marriage or minor ones about a petty argument. The only requirement is that they still bug you from time to time. Then, go through each item and ask yourself, What good came out of this? What was the gift in this? How did I grow as a person because of this? Reframing each regret as a gift is a great way of spinning events in your life as positive rather than negative influences. And once you've done this, it's that much easier to embrace your regrets, be thankful for them and let them go.

* * *

DIG DEEPER

Free Will – This short book by Sam Harris is the best there is on the subject: https://www.samharris.org/free-will

What Neuroscience Says About Free Will – Article by Adam Bear on free will: https://blogs.scientificamerican.com/mind-guest-blog/what-neuroscience-says-about-free-will/

You Don't Have Free Will – Recorded lecture by Larry Coyne on free will: https://www.youtube.com/watch?v=Ca7i-D4ddaw

Free Will Is An Illusion – Video using voice over by Sam Harris: https://vimeo.com/103425310

Free Will Is An Illusion. So What? – Article by Texas professor, Raj Raghunathan:
https://www.psychologytoday.com/blog/sapient-nature/201205/free-will-is-illusion-so-what

STEP SEVEN
THE IMAGINARY PEDESTAL

"Don't look at me in that tone of voice."
– Dorothy Parker

Imagine you're on a train sitting opposite a young woman. She has unwashed blue hair, piercings and tattoos everywhere, and isn't wearing any makeup. A few moments later, she takes off a Dr Marten boot and starts picking her toenails. You get off at your stop and make your way to your old school where there's a reunion taking place. After mingling for a bit, you wind up talking to an old friend you haven't spoken to in over a decade. He tells you he still lives at home with his parents and is a virgin. Later that night, you're lying in bed with a new girlfriend and conversation turns to her sexual history. She tells you that right before you came along she had five friends-with-benefits on the go at once.

Now take a moment to consider what kind of thoughts might have been running through your mind during each of these encounters. How would you describe them later to a friend? Would you be able to talk about the girl on the train, the old friend at the reunion, or your new girlfriend's sex life without saying anything negative? Or making a joke at the other person's expense? If not then congratulations! — you're one of ninety-nine percent of the population who pass judgment on people and things every single day. But don't worry, I'm not passing judgment on your being judgmental.

The reason why so many of us judge is because it feels perfectly natural to do so. And the reason why it feels natural is because it's not only been hardwired into us through evolution, but is also condoned by society. It definitely took me a while to get my head into a less judgmental space, but having done so I can safely say I feel freer as a person and much less critical of myself.

All of which has ultimately helped alleviate my midlife crisis. So, in this step I want to take a look at how unhealthy being judgmental is, how it's fueling your midlife crisis, and what you can do to help repress it.

WHAT'S WRONG WITH BEING JUDGMENTAL?

Let's say you tell a close friend about the girl on the train and call her "disgusting". Then you describe the guy at the reunion as "a loser", and finally your new girlfriend as "a bit slutty". Sure, maybe you're being a tad judgmental, but really what's the harm? Well, the first problem I'd like to point out with judgment is that it's a product of the ego, and so straight away you know you're in trouble.

When you negatively judge other things or people, it's not your true self talking, it's your ego. It's the ego's way of maintaining a Me vs. Them dichotomy which feeds its deception of being superior to that which is being judged. By saying, He's such a loser, for example, what you're really saying is, I'm superior to him and therefore have power over him. By thinking, How could she have had five guys on the go at once, what you're really thinking is, Why doesn't she share my superior moral outlook? By saying, *Boyhood* is the most boring film ever made, you're stating a fact. I'm kidding. What you're really expressing is a personal opinion masquerading as a fact.

Judgment is the product of nasty ego-fueled emotions such as disgust, fear, anger, jealousy and envy, and at its core is an element of dissatisfaction with the way things are. Something or someone is not as it should be, and so the ego feels it has the right to judge, criticize and condemn. This results in a momentary feeling of superiority — a fleeting egoic psychological boost — but the overall longterm effect is that you feel less rather than more happy. By letting your ego continually judge, label, and stereotype everything it sees, you're letting it fill you with negativity and resist reality — the way things really are.

The flip-side of all of this is that ultimately those who judge are more likely to feel judged by others, and in turn to judge themselves. Have a think about how often you self-judge by saying to yourself things like:

- Why do I look so awful in photos? I hate my face.
- There's no point asking her out. Why would she want to go out with me?
- I'm surprised I haven't been fired already, seeing how useless I am at my job.
- Why did I say that? I'm such an idiot.
- I'll never be happy. There must be something wrong me.

Being judgmental about yourself and how you're coming across to other people, leads to becoming unsure of yourself, which deteriorates self-confidence. This lack of self-confidence then results in even more poor self-judgment, and so the cycle continues. Continual self-judgment like this is the cause of much unhappiness because it's the diametric opposite to self-love and awareness. It restricts an ability to be free, fully express yourself and live life on your own terms, not on others.

HOW TO RELINQUISH JUDGMENT

Letting go of judgment is a tough skill to master, however it's not impossible and with practice can be entirely eliminated from your mind. Let's take a look at five things to remember in order to stop being so judgmental of others, and in turn of yourself:

Judgment is only an opinion. As I said in Step Two, your ego has a very black and white view of the world, which means that when you judge yourself or others it's expressed not as a point of view, but as a certainty. There are no room for ifs or buts when it comes to judgment, but like everything to do with the ego, it's an illusion — a story the mind tells itself. Realize, therefore, that when you judge you're expressing a personal opinion wrapped in the illusion of certainty and hard facts. You may *feel* like the girl picking her toenails on the train was disgusting, but always remember that this is an opinion, formed via your upbringing, genetic makeup, societal norms, and a whole host of other nebulous reasons. There is no right or wrong. Only what already "is".

If there is no free will, there can be no judgment. If, as previously discussed, there is no such thing as free will, why be judgmental of other people's actions? Or your own for that matter? If your old school friend is still living at his parents' house due to forces outside of his control, is it really fair to mock or condemn him? Realizing that we don't have free will in the traditional sense opens up a whole new world of compassion and understanding, and is the perfect antidote to judgment.

Learn to discern and accept rather than judge and condemn. Discernment means perceiving the way things are. Judgment means adding resistance and dissatisfaction on top of discernment in order to make a comparison. So learn how to step back from an emotional, judgmental reactions and discern and accept them instead. The two should feel very different. Being judgmental may feel momentarily satisfying but it's rooted in negative emotions. Discernment, on the other hand, simply feels *aware.* The ego feeds off resistance and so naturally can't stand acceptance, but the result should be that even if you're not super enthusiastic about something, you're able to accept what "is" and stop fighting it.

Would you want the world to be boring? Here's a great way to remember not to be judgmental: think to yourself, Would I really want everybody to be just like me? When you judge people it's according to your own values and view of the world, but everyone else's are totally unique to them. Therefore it's unreasonable to expect everyone to be like us, or to *want* everyone to be like us. Personally I don't understand why ninety-percent of modern music is so popular, but that doesn't mean I wish everyone liked exactly the same music as I do because that would be boring. If we all had the same interests, dressed the same, talked the same, etc. we may not feel the need to judge, but we'd be too bored to get out of bed.

Look at judgment as an opportunity for growth. Remember the episode of *Friends* when Ross meets Rachel's new boyfriend and can't stand him, even though he's virtually a clone of himself? To some degree that's what's happening when you judge other people. Because you're not yet fully self-aware, you'd rather see "negative" personality traits in others rather than in yourself. However, by becoming aware of this, judgment can be turned into self-growth when you start to understand others and your judgement towards them as not being something separate from yourself — part of the egoic "Me vs. Them" dichotomy. Rather, see judging other's "faults" as an aspect of judging your own, and this will help stem the need to criticize and condemn.

Here's a practical exercise you can try: don't judge anything or anyone for a day and see how you feel. Then try three days, a week, a month. Whenever you feel the urge to judge, take a step back and simply discern the person or situation without getting emotionally drawn into it. The art of meditation is a great way to practice this too, as already discussed.

Overall, you could go through your days judging other things and people in a million different ways if you were to let your ego loose to run the show. But this isn't a healthy way to move through life as you'll only hurt your self-awareness, self-confidence and wind up with a pretty negative view of the world. And no one likes to be around someone who's always complaining, right? So rather than unconsciously letting your ego delight in putting down others, let your self-awareness help move you toward greater happiness.

STEP EIGHT

IT ALL STARTS WITHIN

"Nothing, she already has Zlatan."
– Zlatan Ibrahimovic when asked what he's getting his wife for her birthday.

Men who fall into midlife crises are often also consumed by comparing themselves to other men, and coming off second best. If you're not one of these guys and are a super confident individual, you can probably skip this section. On the other hand, if you think on some level you're maybe a little insecure within yourself, keep reading.

Remember the saying "You have to love yourself before you can love someone else"? Yes, it annoys me too. However, battling a midlife crisis means starting to value yourself more, recognizing your strengths and weaknesses and accepting yourself for who you are — both the good and the bad. Learn to love yourself instead of judge yourself. Learn to not be so hard on yourself for your own failings or "bad" choices made in the past. This changing of your perception of yourself from maybe a slightly negative one to a more positive one could be one of the most important things you do in your fight against a midlife crisis. From "I don't really respect myself" to "I totally respect everything about myself". From "Good things don't happen to me" to "Great things are going to happen to me". From "My life sucks" to "My life's fantastic". But how do you do this?

There's a ton of information out there on improving self-esteem that I don't have the space here to go into, but I will be talking about health, exercise and nurturing the mind in Step Eleven. The good news, though, is that you can also go about actively addressing self-confidence by changing both your thoughts and your actions.

CHANGE YOUR ACTIONS

Is there something specific you can pinpoint as a cause of your insecurity? Write down all the ways you feel inadequate somehow and what you don't respect about yourself. List all the things you judge about yourself and the things you wish you were. Maybe you don't think you earn enough money? Or you worry that you're overweight? Or underweight?

Have a good hard think about what it is about yourself that you're not so confident about and then get to work tackling it.

Anything you write down in this list is what needs to be tackled head on, through action. Once you do, you'll find your midlife crisis begin to feel more insignificant the more confident you become.

STOP WISHING YOU WERE SOMEONE ELSE

Some guys actually go as far as wishing they were someone else other than themselves. Their reasoning goes something like this: "David Beckham's better looking than me." "Denzel Washington's more charismatic than me." "Ben Stiller's funnier than me." If you're one of these guys, then today is the day you quit this way of thinking. It's unhealthy, nonsensical and ultimately destructive.

It'd probably be quite nice to be able to circumnavigate reality and have Beckham's looks, Denzel's charisma and Ben Stiller's comic timing, but given the opportunity would you really want to exchange places and actually *be* them? Would you want their taste in clothes? Or food? Or women? Would you want their hang-ups? Would you want to actually leave your life and take on theirs? Probably not. Similarly, when you look at that twenty-two-year-old guy on the street with a beautiful girlfriend and feel a tinge of envy, would you really want to be him? So he's twenty-two and has his whole life ahead of him. So what? No matter how great his life may look on the outside, always remember that you're better off being you than somebody else.

CHANGE YOUR THOUGHTS

Simply thinking certain thoughts repeatedly every day is a surprisingly effective way of making you actually believe them. By telling yourself every day that you're a confident person and truly deserve the life you want to lead, your mind will begin to take on these attributes.

Here are a couple of personal statements I want you to write down:

I'm wonderful. Start by writing down a personal statement about how wonderful you are, or a list of all your best qualities — all the things you're good at and all the reasons why your friends and family love you. Really go to town describing how unique and special you are and all your amazing qualities. Imbibe these good vibrations about yourself (maybe through meditation), memorize them and repeat them to yourself as often as possible. Change the way you think about yourself and pretty soon you'll discover the "importance" of past events and future problems will begin to dissolve and lose their significance.

Who do I want to become? Sure you may be wonderful, but there's always room for improvement. Without a clear idea of where you're going, it's hard to know how to get there. So in this second personal statement I want you to write down exactly the kind of man you want to become. Would you like to be more assertive? Make more money? Meet a gorgeous woman? Reconnect with your kids? Be more generous with your time or money? Whatever it is put it down and this will become the blueprint that enables you to clearly visualize just what kind of man you'd like to be.

* * *

DIG DEEPER

How To Be More Confident Than Anyone You Know – Five effective tips in a video by Thomas Frank:
https://www.youtube.com/watch?v=IjB-JRU-_dY

The Skill Of Self Confidence – Ivan Joseph gives an impressive TED talk on how to build self confidence:
https://www.youtube.com/watch?v=w-HYZv6HzAs

How To Have Self Confidence – Part of a Tony Robbins seminar on how to take control of your inner state:
https://www.youtube.com/watch?v=ezSkpyuhymk

The Art Of Loving Yourself – Article by dating supremo, David Wygant: http://www.davidwygant.com/blog/the-art-of-loving-yourself

How To Be More Confident – Leo Gura goes into a step-by-step process for becoming truly confident:
https://www.youtube.com/watch?v=WZmUMRAN-qc

STEP NINE

THE BIG TUNE UP

"Evolution has meant that our prefrontal lobes are too small, our adrenal glands are too big, and our reproductive organs apparently designed by committee; a recipe which, alone or in combination, is very certain to lead to some unhappiness and disorder."
– Christopher Hitchens

As we age, it can sometimes become harder to keep our minds and bodies in shape. Work, family and a general lack of time and energy, often means we end up slipping into bad eating habits and a sedentary lifestyle, and before we know it we're unable to carry a crate of beers into the house without needing to lie down. An unhealthy lifestyle, however, can not only harm your body and mind, but also your self-confidence, productivity and overall happiness. One of the best things you can do while navigating the choppy waters of a midlife crisis, is to give your body and mind a tune up. In this step, therefore, I'll be covering the three key areas of: diet, exercise and mental sharpness.

Don't worry, I'm not here to give you a lecture on how you need to turn into a teetotal kale munching gym bunny. But if you think you could be healthier than you are at the moment, it's worth doing something about it, no matter how small. If you're already a health nut who's been on a paleo diet for a year and has ten percent body fat, however, you can probably go ahead and skip this section. If not, let's kick off with some...

FOOD FOR THOUGHT

Let's face it, most of us know we should be eating healthier but struggle to ever put it into practice. Diets are began and promptly dropped after a few weeks when we fail to see any significant results, don't feel much better and can't stand the thought of another day eating something called "bone broth". Sticking to the latest crash diet like this, in which you're supposed to religiously count calories or cut out carbs, can be virtually impossible. Even the people who find some success and actually lose weight, often end up putting it back on and feeling even worse than they did beforehand. Not to mention all the confusion that's out there on what you should and shouldn't be consuming. One minute turning vegan is the best thing you can possibly do, the next it causes cancer.

While diets that completely revolutionize your eating habits obviously work for some, I wasn't one of them. Instead, I found it easier to keep eating what I liked, but less of it. That meant smaller portions and sometimes skipping meals such as breakfast or lunch altogether. If you feel there's something you're going overboard with eating, now might be the time to tone it down. Make a list of foodstuffs, such as meat, sweets, alcohol, etc. that you may be consuming too much of, and start consuming less. Or set yourself a challenge to give something up for a month, one at a time. The monthly schedule will not only give you a motivational goal to work toward, but also train your body to live without whatever it is you want to cut down on.

After thirty days, you should find it easier to consume it more moderately. For example, after years of snacking on sweets and cakes throughout the day, I gave them up for a month and now only treat myself to something sweet on the weekend. Breaking down the week like this is another way of making cutting down on certain foodstuffs easier, as it works on a hardship/reward framework. It's not so galling to turn down a donut on a Wednesday if you know you can have one on Saturday.

If you want to give a structured diet a go, however, I suggest checking out some of the resources in the Dig Deeper section below, where I list several guys who can help you out.

Overall, I would strongly recommend taking the steps now to improve your diet or else risk running into problems later in life that maybe could've been avoided. I'm not saying you have to turn into Gwyneth Paltrow, but start giving your body more of the right kind of fuel and it will thank you for it. What we eat obviously has a major part to play in how healthy our bodies are. But did you know just how big a role it plays in keeping our brains healthy too? While reading *The UltraMind Solution* by Mark Hyman, I was struck by the following section:

Serotonin: staying happy

Do you have low serotonin levels? Take the following quiz to find out. In the box on the right, place a check for each positive answer. Then find out how severe your problem is by using the scoring key below.

Serotonin quiz

- My head is full of ANTS (automatic negative thoughts).
- I'm a glass half empty person.
- I have low self esteem and self confidence.
- I tend to have obsessive thoughts and behaviors.
- I get the winter blues or have SAD (seasonal affective disorder.)
- I tend to be irritable, easily angered, and / or impatient.

- I am shy and afraid of going out, or have a fear of heights, crowds, flying, and / or public speaking.
- I feel anxious and have panic attacks.
- I have trouble falling asleep.
- I wake up in the middle of the night and have trouble getting back to sleep, or wake up too early.
- I crave sweets or starchy carbs like bread and pasta.
- I feel better when I exercise.
- I have muscle aches, fibromyalgia, and / or jaw pain (TMJ.)
- I have been treated with and felt better when taking SSRIs (serotonin boosting antidepressants.)

Scoring Key

Score one point for each box you checked.

Score Severity

0 – 4   You may have a slightly low level of serotonin.

5 – 7   You may have a moderately low level of serotonin.

8+   You may have a severely low level of serotonin.

If you scored highly on the test and are someone who doesn't take that much care of what they eat, this lifestyle is probably helping to fuel your midlife crisis without you even realizing it. So, especially if your crisis is particularly bad, maybe have a go at completing the six week program in the book. Mark Hyman explains exactly how to increase your serotonin and decrease your stress levels by introducing things like magnesium, vitamin B6, tryptophan and protein to your diet, while eliminating anything with high sugar content, allergies, infections and toxins.

LET'S GET PHYSICAL

If the thought of changing your diet was bad enough, how about the prospect of taking up regular exercise? If you didn't leap up and down at the prospect, shouting "Yes, let's do this!", don't worry, I fully understand. We're middle-aged guys, and a vast number of us haven't exercised in any meaningful way for years, so it's perfectly natural to feel a little nauseous at the thought of starting now. Engaging in a sport or joining a gym can be an expensive, boring and fairly obnoxious experience. And besides, where are you supposed to find the time?

However, the problem lies in the fact that as we progress into middle age, our cardio-vascular system becomes less effective. We begin to lose more and more muscle tone and replace with fat. We lose our strength and endurance, meaning it becomes easier to tear and strain ligaments and muscles. And our bones become porous and brittle as they lose calcium, again increasing the risk of fracture.

In short, if we continue on into our middle-age with a less than active lifestyle, we put ourselves at risk of a whole host of health problems in the present and further on down the line. The good news is, though, that much of this depressing physical decline can be considerably slowed or even fully reversed by starting to exercise.

It's been scientifically proven, for example, that people who do regular physical activity have:

- Up to an 83% lower risk of arthritis
- Up to a 68% lower risk of hip fracture
- Up to a 50% lower risk of type 2 diabetes
- Up to a 50% lower risk of colon cancer
- Up to a 35% lower risk of coronary heart disease and stroke
- Up to a 30% lower risk of depression
- Up to a 30% lower risk of dementia
- Up to a 30% lower risk of early death

As well as the above benefits, regular exercise also reduces the risk of obesity, improves bone health and muscular/ cardiorespiratory fitness, keeps us flexible, lowers stress levels, raises energy and mood levels and improves sleep patterns. Exercise also has a major positive impact on the mind, much in the same way as what we choose to eat. By releasing serotonin and other soothing chemicals such as dopamine, regular physical activity kills stress, boosts and improves connections between nerve cells, releases tension and acts as a natural anti-depressant.

But how do you suddenly start exercising again after fifteen years? Firstly, if you're not that way inclined, I'd avoid engaging in anything you don't actually enjoy on some level, like going to the gym or jogging round the block. You'll just get bored and frustrated and give up. (Running is probably the worst kind of exercise someone our age could do anyway, if you consider the impact damage to your knees and hips.) So, I'd recommend doing something you actually enjoy, such as swimming, cycling or a sport with a friend.

Whatever form of exercise you choose, aim to increase your endurance levels and the performance of your heart through cardiovascular aerobic exercise. In general, you can consider yourself minimally fit if you can increase your heart rate to at least 100 beats per minute and keep it there for half an hour, for a period of twenty minutes daily or forty-five minutes three times a week. Ideally, aim to raise your heart rate to at least sixty percent of your maximum pulse rate — that is, the top speed your heart can beat and still pump blood around your body. Your maximum heart rate is 220 less your age. So if you're, say, forty-five, you should aim for an exercise heart rate of 105 (220 - 45 = 180 x 0.6 = 105).

If you can't abide the thought of playing football, squash or swimming, how about walking? In fact, this is probably one of the very best forms of exercise for middle-aged men as it enables you to get fit, measure your progress and listen to your favorite music or podcast at the same time. I'm not talking about ambling along, though. I'm talking about really walking at a pace — say a mile under fifteen minutes — and increasing your speed the fitter you get. If you walk two miles in half an hour, five times a week, you'll be engaging in a healthy fitness regime that's totally free and easy.

Regarding those ailing muscles I mentioned earlier, aim to also lightly increase your body strength via muscle resistance exercises, such as push-ups, pull-ups and sit-ups and/or working with weights. But don't go overboard. Forget the mantra "No pain, no gain" for now or you'll probably put yourself in ER, especially if you haven't done much physical activity in a while. Start slowly and gradually begin to build up your workout regimen as your body acclimatizes to suddenly moving about more. And don't forget to remain flexible by stretching thoroughly before any form of physical activity, or by practicing yoga.

The great thing is, you don't need to join a gym anymore to start this kind of training. It can be done using little more than a workout mat and a laptop in the comfort of your own home, and I include some great resources at the end of this step regarding this. But remember to check out the latest research findings and your doctor's recommendations before embarking on any form of repetitive exercise program.

I realize how hard it can be to commit to regular physical activity like this, but it will result in tremendous long term health benefits. After incorporating a regular exercise program into my week, for example, I soon felt much more energized. In the afternoon when normally I could be found lightly dozing face down on my keyboard, I felt much more "with it". And my self-confidence grew too.

The biggest excuse to not exercise is often a lack of time, but given the benefits can you really afford to skip out on it now and risk running into problems later in life? Research has proved again and again that those middle-aged beer bellies are hiding much more than just a six-pack. They're a sign of potentially more serious problems that can affect a person later on in life. Researchers at Boston University, for example, found that men who failed to do much physical activity in their forties wound up with smaller brain volumes in their sixties. I'm not trying to scare you, but we're talking about three to six hours physical activity a week, which is hardly an inordinate amount of time when it comes to looking after your most precious commodity — your health.

THE MIND

According to the latest Nielsen Report on how much time each week we all spend watching TV, we're all doing far too much of it. Here's the weekly average time middle-aged Americans spend in front of the TV:

Age 35 to 49: 33 hours, 40 minutes
Age 50 to 64: 43 hours, 56 minutes

That's an awful lot of TV. A full time job, in fact. And that's not even counting all the gazing we do at other types of screens, such as computers and mobile devices. The British, apparently, spend more hours a day on their laptops and fiddling with their phones than they do asleep. Eight hours and forty-one minutes to be exact. While there's nothing intrinsically wrong with watching TV, or using phones and laptops, the key word here again is *moderation*. I haven't got the space here to go into all the health problems associated with excessive use of these devices, but I will say that maybe this behavior is exacerbating your midlife crisis.

In general, if you're spending more time during the day engaging with a screen than real life, then it's probably time to reassess your habits.

Here are three ways to get started today:

Cut down on the TV. If you're watching ten different shows each week, or tend to loll around on the couch just watching whatever comes on, maybe it's time to be a bit more ruthless when it comes to what get beams into your house. Personally I've never seen *Game of Thrones*, *Breaking Bad*, *The Wire* or whatever show is currently hot at the moment, so maybe I'm not the best qualified person to talk about this, but I'm pretty sure they're not all "required viewing". Give your viewing habits a review and see what can be ditched in order to get your total time spent watching TV down to twenty hours a week or lower.

Turn off your phone. I don't know what's happened to our society but it seems no one can get through ten minutes anymore without checking their cell phone: talking to friends/family, walking down the street, driving, waiting on a street corner, going to sleep, waking up, watching a film *in a movie theater*... If this sounds like you, it's time to look up, put your shoulders back, take in your surroundings and start interacting with the world again. You're missing out on a million potential conversations when your head's buried in your phone. (With women too, if you're single.)

Step away from the computer. Sitting in a swivel chair staring at a computer screen is the default pose for many of us at work, but according to many studies the damaging effects on the body are as harmful as smoking. Sitting for just six hours a day leads to all kinds of scary problems such as loss of bone mass, bad posture, muscle atrophy, weight gain, higher cholesterol, heart disease and cancer. The good news, however, is that much of this can be mitigated by getting up and moving about every so often. Set an alarm to go off every hour and make sure you fully stretch your legs to get the circulation going again. A ten minute break per sitting hour is recommended but may not be practical, but aim to get up and move about as often as you can.

* * *

DIG DEEPER

HASfit – At home workouts for guys of all fitness levels, and they're free: http://hasfit.com/which-program-is-right-for-me/

The Diet Myth – Book by Tim Spector that shows how the key to health isn't which foods we eat but the microbes in our guts: http://www.tim-spector.co.uk/the-diet-myth/

Spark – Book by John Ratey on the revolutionary new science of exercise and its effect on the brain: http://www.johnratey.com/Books.php

Abs Over Forty – This get-fit program is designed specifically for men who are middle aged: https://sixpackshortcuts.com/desktop/absafter40

Insanity Sixty Day Challenge – If you're up for it, Shaun T's workout is guaranteed to get your body in the best shape of its life: http://bchbody.life/2fDWOXa

STEP TEN

IS THIS IT?

"The two most important days in your life are the day you are born and the day you find out why."
– Mark Twain

Often, guys in the grip of a midlife crisis react to their feelings of ennui and life frustrations by "acting out" and making big, life-changing decisions concerning their work and relationships. Drastic and often destructive measures are taken, such as jobs being quit, careers being changed, partners being dumped, and divorce proceedings being instigated. These actions arise from reaching middle-age and, basically, panicking. Life's half over, and yet it feels like a failure. This results in an overpowering urge to "shake things up" and take a different, more exciting path "before it's too late". A desire like this usually evolves into fantasies of affairs with much younger women, fast cars, motorbikes and road trips, or quitting a boring job to pursue an unfulfilled life-long passion.

Is leaving your job or your wife sometimes the very best thing you should do? And if so, what's the best way to do it? Or should you do nothing, suffer through your male midlife crisis in silence and wait for the U-shaped curve to start heading upward at an unspecified time in the future? In order to answer these questions and more, I'm going to take a look at each of the ways men act out during a male midlife crisis in turn:

- Making big work/career changes
- Making big marriage/longterm relationship changes

MAKING A BIG WORK CHANGE

Many men find themselves feeling bored and trapped by their employment circumstances. Bills need to be paid, mouths need to be fed, and so on. Despite this, a desire to pull a Lester Burnham, stick two fingers up at your boss and make a drastic career or life change can become overwhelming. This often boils down to a dichotomy between doing a job that satisfies materially but leaves you feeling empty, or quitting it in order to finally do what you love but not having any financial security. The best way to approach your midlife crisis and work, though, is to take a step back and break down where you are exactly employment-wise, where you'd like to be, and what realistic steps could you take to get there.

Here are five steps you can take to improve your work situation:

Step 1: Work out your current career's pros and cons

If you're toying with the idea of changing your career, the first step is to work out what you want to change and why. Start by making a list of all the reasons why you'd really love to hand in that resignation letter on Monday morning. (Or if you're self-employed, would love to hand it over to yourself.) Are your colleagues unbearable? Does your commute take two and half hours each way? Is the work itself boring as hell? Whatever the reasons, put them down but be sure to include things that may not only be detrimental to you, but to your family and friends.

Next, write down what you *like* about your current position. Granted, this may be a short list, but try to think of some things that you'd miss if you were to quit tomorrow. Now really analyze your answers in order to nail down which aspects of your career you'd want to bring along to your next job, and which you'd happily leave behind. This will all be highly valuable info once you start thinking about what you really want to do in Step 2.

Regarding what aspects you'd like to keep, however, make sure it's definitely the career itself that's causing your malaise, and not factors that can possibly be remedied, such as work colleagues, particular job position, company you work for, etc.

On reflection, you might discover that by making a few changes to your current role things would be okay. For example, you could ask for a pay rise, move closer to work, transfer to another office, take up a different position within the same company, etc.

If you're still certain you need to make a more drastic change, though, it's time to have a think about what this might entail.

Step 2: Decide if you want to give it all up to "follow your passion"

If you've always had a burning desire to be a novelist, direct movies, or open your own *Pulp Fiction*-themed restaurant, now might be the perfect time to try and make that dream a reality. To be middle-aged is, after all, still far from being old, and an argument could be made for giving it a shot now before it's too late. A common argument for doing this is to "follow your passion". Blog posts, YouTube videos, and books are all full of experts and lay people alike telling us to "never give up on the dream" and "pursue your passion" because "you only live once". "Why spend your whole life waking up every morning to go to a job you hate, when you could leap out of bed, super amped to fulfill your childhood passion?" goes the argument.

While this advice is well-intentioned, it's also fraught with some hidden perils that are worth checking out before you hand in your notice. Firstly, the advice to "follow your dream" is simplistic and overly optimistic. It implies that all you need do is follow a pre-existing, burning desire inside you to paint, write, act, become a marine biologist or whatever it is, and then never give up until you make it. However, having a passion for something doesn't necessarily mean that by sticking to it forever you're going to make it. Or that your passion naturally goes hand-in-hand with actually being good at it in the first place, as should be obvious to anyone who's ever seen five minutes of *The X-Factor*.

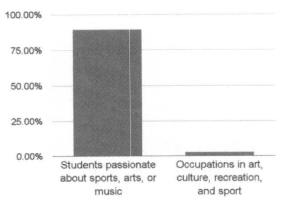

Passions vs. Jobs

University of Montreal and Canadian Census Data

As a matter of fact, being "good" is far from enough. Due to the high levels of competition surrounding most "dream jobs" whether they're creative or not, you'll need to be *exceptional*. Here's a study conducted at a University of Montreal which clearly demonstrates this disconnect between passion and career prospects:

Secondly, let's say you get that dream job after following your passion, there's no guarantee you're actually going to like it. Our passions and "gut instincts" are often prone to leading us astray, as well as fooling us into thinking their permanent when they're not. What you were passionate about ten years ago you may no longer care for, and what you're passionate about now, may not interest you in ten years time. Likewise, let's say you've always had a dream to write screenplays professionally, but when you actually get hired to write one, may realize the stress involved of hustling gigs, pitching at meetings, uncertain pay checks, and constantly having your work rewritten, etc. is too much to handle.

That's not to say that pursuing your passion is *always* a bad idea, but it will inevitably come with an element of risk. If you're determined to make a change, though, I have a few points for you to consider shortly in Step 3.

But what if you don't have a passion in the first place? The advice to "follow your heart" presumes everyone has a pre-existing, intense enthusiasm for something already inside them, just waiting to be let loose on the world. But what if you're one of many men who find themselves trapped in boring, unfulfilling jobs but have no real idea of what they'd rather be doing instead?

You may only have one strong skill-set — to do the job you're already doing — and so the thought of doing anything else might be hard to imagine. However, now could be a great time to consider some options.

Stay in your career or job but make some changes. Work out what it would it take for you to be happier in your career. Is there a different role you could take on within the same company? Is there a way you could be trained up in order to branch out? Is there another office you could transfer to in a different city or country that'd give your career a new lease of life? This may not be the sexiest option out there, but if some peace can be found by making a few changes, it's probably the easiest.

Brainstorm potential passions. The truth is, passions don't always just arrive within us fully formed. They grow as we improve our skills in a particular field. Steve Jobs, for example, didn't start out with a burning desire to conquer the world of personal computing — he stumbled into it as a way to make some quick cash and *then* got hooked. So, make a list of all the broad areas you wouldn't mind working in, that you think you may have some aptitude for, and then build from there. What are you good at? How could you help other people? What changes would you like to make to your local community? What causes really get you going? How do you think you could find more meaning in your work life? It's these kind of questions that should lead you to discovering what kind of work you'll end up being passionate about a little further on down the road.

Zero in on your top three. Once you have a list of possible ideas, put them in a top three list and then have a think about all the ways you could get started with number one. Cultivating a passion could be a slow process, so it's a case of starting with your top choice, seeing where it leads, and moving on to the next if it doesn't work out. Could you enroll on evening classes, a bachelor/masters degree pr PhD? Or get a part-time job in your chosen field? Or set up your own online business during evenings and weekends? Check out some of Chris Guillebeau's books for some great advice on repositioning a career once you're middle-aged.

Step 3: Figure out the best ways to minimize risk

Whether you already have a passion, or need to do some work first on working out what it could be, switching careers during midlife will probably involve some short-term hardships and a hit to your finances. That's why it's important to make sure you're financially prepared before going ahead, and don't shoot yourself in the foot. Here are some options:

Downsize your home. Sell up and buy something smaller, giving you access to funds and the chance to build your business, search for a new job, or return to study.

Downsize your job. Sacrifice some of your salary by going part-time. Or quit and take a more flexible job that will enable you to focus on your new career goals.

Expenses audit. Keep track of all your expenses for a couple of months, then work out how much you'd need to be able to live on without a steady income. Then save up that amount before quitting or downsizing your job.

Use equity. If you're a homeowner, consider taking out equity on it as a means of raising funds for your period of exploration.

Emergency fund. Work out what you'd do if you had some unexpected expenses to take care of. Where would you find the money?

Step 4: Draw up an action plan

Let's say you have a passion you want to pursue (or a potential one you want to cultivate), and have savings in the bank. The next step is to draw up an action plan with a specific set of goals that you want to achieve. The danger otherwise is that with too much free time on your hands your vision may become hazy and unfocused. Decide how long you want to give your new project before reassessing whether it's worth quitting, staying the course, or trying something new. This deadline shouldn't necessarily mean you should have "made it" by the end, but that you'll have reached a significant milestone of some kind. If you want to be a novelist, for example, you'll want to have written a book before the deadline and had some feedback on it from someone in the business, like an author, editor, or literary agent.

Let's say you've decided to dedicate a year to this goal. The best way to structure the year would be to divide it into three month chunks and have a different mini goal at the end of March, June, September, and December. And then further subdivide each three month mini-goal into weekly micro goals. This is a much better approach than coming up with a new goal every day as some productivity gurus advocate. We all know what it's like to have a list of five daily goals, and then only three get done and so two spill over into the next day, and so on. The key is to not make your goals too difficult so you just get frustrated and give up. Going back to the novelist analogy for a moment — aiming to write forty pages a week is far easier than aiming to write ten pages a day. Other commitments are bound to get in the way, but if you know you have a whole week to accomplish something you can organize your time that much more effectively.

Step 5: Make the commitment

Fear of the unknown may well have been holding you back from making any career changes before now. But if you've worked out what work you're passionate about and what will give you a sense of purposefulness and meaning to your life, then it's time to make a commitment to it.

The way to do this is to first push past any remaining fears, doubts and uncertainties you may be holding on to by asking yourself, "In the future, will I regret not giving this a go?" Picture yourself as an older man, fifteen or twenty years from now. Will you look back on this period in your life and wish you'd had the balls to give it a shot? If you think the answer might be "yes", then it's probably worth going through some hardships now in order to reap the benefits later of a new career that you actually enjoy.

MAKING A BIG RELATIONSHIP CHANGE

As well as feeling an overwhelming need to make big career changes, a midlife crisis can also have a similar effect on relationships. Here are the most common symptoms associated with having a male midlife crisis when it comes to relationships:

Feeling trapped: Many men feel stuck in their longterm relationships — like there's no way out because of shared circumstances such as kids, finances, a long shared history, etc. Or simply being fearful of winding up alone.

Lack of validation: Your partner no longer makes you feel special, attractive, or wanted. Whereas once you felt like you were the center of their universe, now it seems you're behind her friends, family and the cat.

Lack of excitement: Having been with the same person for many years, things may not be as exciting as when you first met. Feelings of ennui and boredom can become overwhelming as you struggle to find anything interesting about her anymore.

Lack of communication: Not feeling like you can talk to your partner because they've stopped listening or caring. Which leads to…

Internal suffering: Concerns about the relationship are bottled up because you feel you can't talk about them with your partner. Which in turn makes your partner more uneasy and suspicious of you and so the problems spiral.

Identity crisis: As your midlife crisis progresses, you're changing but leaving your partner behind. Confusion, self-doubt, and fear set in, causing you to reevaluate your relationship and wonder whether it's worth staying in.

Work out which came first: your relationship problems or your midlife crisis

If you're experiencing some or all of the above symptoms in your relationship, the first thing to do is work out if they're due to your male midlife crisis or if you'd have them anyway. Many marriages fail during midlife, but not all as a result of a midlife crisis. Take some time out to really analyze your situation. Do you think you're unhappy in your relationship because you're going through a midlife crisis? Or do you think it would be fine if the crisis didn't exist?

As you maybe know, staying happy in a longterm relationship can be tricky, but working out in your own mind how much of a role your midlife crisis is playing is an important first step. Assuming you believe your relationship problems are in fact due to your midlife crisis, it's time to work out what to do about them.

Is it time to make some big relationship changes?

Many men who suffer from a midlife crisis feel an overwhelming need to "shake things up" in their relationship and instigate some kind of big change. Here are the three main changes most men opt for:

- Have an affair/flings/hook-ups
- Take a break from the relationship
- Get divorced/permanently separate

If you're considering engaging in any of the above changes, it means your emotional and/or sexual needs are no longer being met in the relationship. Communication channels with your partner have probably broken down, and feelings bottled up during an intense period of internal suffering.

All of which leads to a need to release pent up emotions by making some big changes in your relationship. Let's take a look at each of these three options in turn by weighing up the pros and cons of each.

AFFAIRS, FLINGS AND HOOK-UPS

While a midlife crisis represents stagnation and the "same-old same-old", an affair represents forward motion and exciting new options. Rather than go on feeling trapped by the same routines, an affair offers many the opportunity to "feel alive once again". The lack of excitement that's been missing in a stale, safe, boring relationship is re-found in abundance with someone new. Emotional and sexual needs are met by having someone to talk to and get excited about physically. A feeling of being wanted and validated returns as you reassure yourself you've "still got it". There's a spring in your step and life feels worth living again.

There's also the chance that your affair won't just be about the thrill of it all and dirty weekends away, but that you might actually end up with your soul mate. An affair can also help springboard couples into action and either end a doomed relationship that's only keeping them miserable, or help rekindle their lost passion. When it's put like that, having an affair may not seem like such a bad idea. But is it? The truth is, having an affair, fling, or cheating in general, rarely works out. Rather, they tend to add problems to an already difficult situation:

Stress. Will your friend remember to say you were both at a work conference last weekend? Is your lover's perfume lingering on your shirt? Will your wife work out your phone's pass code? Keeping an affair going means developing an eye for detail usually found in secret agents, and the stress of being possibly found out can be overwhelming.

Guilt. It's obviously disrespectful to go sneaking around your partner's back, sleeping with someone else and pretending everything's okay when it's not. Is this the kind of man you want to be? If you're able to look in the mirror and feel no guilty conscious at all then maybe so. But guilt is a truly horrible emotion to carry around day in day out.

Non-achievement. Very often an affair means looking for a solution to an unhappy relationship in someone new, when really you should be looking within yourself. This is why many affairs end when problems arise that were there in the old relationship. Old habits reform, the sex gets boring, the conversations dry up and before you know it you're in exactly the same situation you were in before. Very often it's the one having an affair who needs to change, not the partner.

Loss. To have an affair means you have to be very open to the possibility that your partner will find out. And if they find out there's a good chance they'll leave you. If you're having (or are thinking of having) an affair that's based purely on sex, is it worth the risk, considering the fact you probably won't have someone to fall back on? Are you ready to be alone and single as a middle-aged man?

Suffering. If your partner does find out, you will not only be inflicting an enormous amount of pain on them and your kids if you have any, but also on yourself. Again, you have to be willing to hurt others and potentially be disliked for a very long time. Even if you find happiness with your lover, it's not easy to move away from the fact that it's built on the unhappiness of others.

If you're considering having an affair (or are already having one) the first thing to consider is: Do you want to have an affair on the side and keep your partner, or do you want to get out of the relationship for good and be with someone new (or by yourself)? Either way, you're better off being honest with your partner and with yourself. If you want to have an affair on the side, it's best to leave your partner first, because otherwise you're being disrespectful. If you want to get out for good, then get out for good. In both cases, it's a question of manning up and doing what you know is right, rather than what's easiest.

TAKING A BREAK

"I think we should take a break" is probably in the top five most dreaded sentences anyone in a relationship wants to hear. But should it be? The truth is "taking a break" doesn't necessarily mean breaking up. Sometimes people (especially men) just need some space to get a little perspective. Rather than looking at a break as an excuse to go crazy and sleep with as many people as you can, think of it as an opportunity to see the relationship through a fresh set of eyes. A hiatus could give you the chance to consider questions such as: How do I feel now that she's not around? Do I miss her or do I prefer being alone? Am I finding it hard to resist reaching out? Does absence truly make the heart grow fonder, or is my life generally better now than it was before?

If you do end up taking a break from your relationship, make sure you establish some ground rules first. Here are some questions you and your partner might want to consider:

How much contact will you have?: This could range from moving out and not hearing a word from each other, to calling each other from time to time to check in. Work out some rules before you both decide on a break on just how much you want to see or hear of each other.

How long will it last?: Taking a break could mean anything from three weeks to three months, so it's important you're both clear on how long you want it to last. Too short and it might not even feel like a break. Too long and either one of you might grow a little too accustomed to being alone.

Will you see other people?: If so, what does "see" mean. Is kissing allowed? Is having sex allowed? Will you swap stories or not? Personally, I think if you're serious about working things out with your partner, I wouldn't recommend seeing other people while on a break. Finding out details you didn't want to find out could lead to things quickly disintegrating.

What do you want to achieve?: Discuss which aspects of each other's behavior you'd like to change and promise to work on it individually during the break. Otherwise, you may just end up taking a break and then just picking up the same old arguments you had before you left.

Make sure the rules are clearly spelled out and both party understands what "taking a break" actually means. The last thing either of you want to do is turn into Ross from *Friends* — "We were on a break!" If you're both determined to make things work, taking a break could be a good course of action. However, if the relationship is already nearly dead it'll probably just delay the inevitable. Before taking a break always ask yourself, Am I running away from conflicts that'll just reappear once I return? Or do I truly want to gain some perspective and really try and make a change?

THE BIG "D"

Laura had been married for fifteen years when her middle-aged husband, Eddie, began growing more and more distant. Whenever she asked him if anything was wrong he'd say everything's fine — it's just a phase. One day, though, Eddie announced out the blue that he wanted a divorce. He hastily packed a suitcase, jumped into his car and drove off, never to return. Laura, as you can imagine, was left dumbstruck.

This scenario gets played out at an alarmingly frequent rate among middle-aged men who are going through a midlife crisis. Laura was lucky in that at least Eddie had seemed distant before taking off. Some men just walk out without giving away the slightest hint they were unhappy. This kind of impulsive, unpredictable, temperamentally based behavior is often the result of many months or years of bottled up emotions finally being released. While the man may feel a sense of relief, like a huge weight has been lifted from his shoulders, wives and kids are left crushed.

Before deciding on any of these three actions — having an affair, taking a break or getting divorced — try to disconnect your emotions from the situation and think as clearly as possible about the consequences.

Are you sure the relationship is over, or that you're willing to risk it permanently ending? Would trying to talk about how you're feeling again help? Are there any other methods you could try to rekindle the spark you once had?

Freshen up the relationship. Have you tried to rekindle the feelings you had when you first met your partner? Ways of doing this include, taking a vacation in your honeymoon destination, going on "dates", reorganizing your routines, giving more time to each other, exchanging romantic gifts, etc.

See things from their perspective. Try to put yourself in their shoes by having a think about all the external influences your partner has had to deal with that makes them act the way they act. If you had experienced exactly the same upbringing from the same parents, lived in the same place, had the same life experiences, would you have acted any differently?

Do some research on free will. Following on from this, reconsider whether free will actually exists. If, as many scientists now believe, free will is an illusion, then all of our actions are the result of neurological impulses that we can't control. In other words, if your partner has no other choice than to behave as they do, and neither do you, then can you really blame them or yourself for your actions?

Try marriage counseling. If all else fails, and you can afford it, try talking to a professional counselor about your differences. Having a neutral party hear both of your grievances could be an effective way of challenging them and putting your relationship back on track.

WHAT'S THE ALTERNATIVE TO MAKING A BIG CHANGE?

If you've been thinking about having an affair, taking a break or getting divorced, chances are you've been bottling up your emotions rather than talking them through with anyone. The trouble is, a suppression of feelings usually leads to either one of the big changes above — with all the problems associated with them — or to giving up and "dying inside".

This can be just as harmful as impulsively acting out and quitting your job or asking for a divorce as it means all the resentment and unhappiness inside you will continue to build and fester but have no outlet. The result being you become a shadow of your former self and never truly enjoy life or reach your full potential.

Here are a few ways you can give your life a renewed sense of purpose without making a big change that's going to drastically affect you or those around you.

Change your routine. A large part of being embroiled in a midlife crisis comes down to feeling trapped and stuck in a routine you can't break out of. Figure out how you can mix things up so your life is not quite so predictable. Is there a club or society you can join once a week? Could you cycle to work instead of drive? Are there any different sorts of people you could start hanging out with?

Pursue your passion. What do you really *enjoy* doing? What activity gives you immense satisfaction in life? Whatever it is, this is what you should be doing more of. Find out what it is that would give the optimum amount of satisfaction — whether that's an on-going pursuit, or a one-off goal — and make sure you do more of it. Every month, week or day.

Write a bucket list. *What do you want to create*? An app. A painting. An online business. *Where do you want to go*? Montreal. The San Siro stadium. Abroad, alone. *Who do you want to be*? A father. A leader. A semi-professional musician. *What do you want to accomplish*? A doctorate. A road trip across the United States. Shake Sam Rockwell's hand. *What do you want to learn*? French. How to surf. A potted history of every country in the world. *What do you want to quit*? Drinking. Refined sugar. Being impatient.

Create a safe space. These shouldn't be reserved just for millennial special snowflakes, but also for middle-aged men.

Take some time out away from everyone every so often to recharge your batteries in a man cave at the bottom of the garden, or a log cabin, or AirBnB apartment, etc.

Quit Facebook. Or at least stop spending so much time on it. Social media sites such as Facebook have been scientifically proven to cause stress as they result in comparing your life everyone else's and coming off second best. A better approach is to worry less about other people's lives and start creating your own memories to last a lifetime.

Overall, a midlife crisis tends to make guys act out in unpredictable and irrational ways, but you don't have to fall victim to your emotions in this way. Rather, take a deep breath and note that you're feeling this way due to emotional and biological changes brought on by midlife. Then take your time to properly consider the consequences of your actions and do what feels right in the long term, not just the short.

* * *

DIG DEEPER

Meet Up – Meet new people, join new clubs, get involved with societies: https://www.meetup.com

Chris Guillebeau – Traveler and best-selling author of *The Art Of Non-Conformity* and *The Happiness Of Pursuit*: http://chrisguillebeau.com/books/

Live Your Legend – Inspirational site founded by the late Scott Dinsmore: http://liveyourlegend.net

Remote Year – Travel the world with seventy-five other people, working remotely: http://www.remoteyear.com

Charles Duhigg – Discover the secrets of being productive in life and business: http://charlesduhigg.com

STEP ELEVEN

THE TWO BEST MEDICINES

"From the moment I picked your book up until I laid it down, I was convulsed with laughter. Someday I intend reading it."
– Groucho Marx

I want you to do these four things, right now. Don't worry, I'll wait for you.

1. Give your current mood a number: 1 being the lowest and 10 the highest.

2. Watch this video: https://goo.gl/1KchVq

3. Listen to this song at full volume: https://goo.gl/3LNcq6

4. Give your mood a number: 1 being the lowest and 10 the highest.

Was the last number you wrote down higher than the first? While you may think the effects of laughing at a funny video or listening to a feel-good song are temporary, here's the strange thing: *the more often you do it, the less temporary the effects.*

THE HEALING POWER OF LAUGHTER

You may not be aware of it but laughing does more for us than just providing us with temporary comic relief. In much the same way as having sex produces various health benefits — ranging from better sleep patterns, to lower stress levels and blood pressure, to increased immunity — laughing has a similar positive effect on the body.

In study after study it's been shown that laughter (and we're talking proper yuks here, not just a light giggle) causes an increase in a whole host of life enhancing properties, including:

- An increase in "natural killer cells" which attack viral infected cells, cancer and tumors
- An increase in activated T cells, which "turn up" the immune system
- An increase in the antibody IgA, which fights respiratory infections
- An increase in gamma interferon, which activates the immune system

- An increase in IgB, the immunoglobulin produced in the greatest quantity in body
- An increase in Complement 3, which helps antibodies to pierce dysfunctional or infected cells

Laughing's great for the fighting dysfunctional cells and the immune system, but studies have also shown that it's also good at decreasing stress hormones, dopamine levels and consequently blood pressure. Again, much like sex, laughter is a form of aerobic workout which increases the body's oxygen functioning. Scientists even believe that when employed alongside conventional care, the positive emotions released by laughter help reduce pain and aid in the healing of diseases.

Here's Norman Cousins, the man who "cured himself of disease through the power of laughter" on the subject:

"I made the joyous discovery that ten minutes of genuine belly laughter had an anesthetic effect and would give me at least two hours of pain-free sleep. When the pain-killing effect of the laughter wore off, my wife and I would switch on the motion picture projector again and not infrequently, it would lead to another pain-free interval."

Way back in 1964, Cousins was given just a few months left to live after being diagnosed with a rare degenerative disease known as Ankylosing Spondylitis. He was left in almost constant pain and was advised by his doctor advised to get his "affairs in order". Cousins, however, was never a man to turn down a challenge, and rather than draw up a will and wait for the inevitable, he instead drew up an action plan to beat the disease himself. The first casualty was his doctor, who was promptly fired and replaced with one who wouldn't interfere as much.

Next, he moved out of hospital and into a hotel, whereupon he set up a movie projector and began administering a high daily dosage of Marx Brothers movies direct to his funny bone. (Luckily, Cousins was unable to get hold of any *Carry On* movies or he may not have survived the week.) His condition steadily improved and within a couple of months he was back on his feet. Two years later he was back at his job as editor-in-chief at the *Saturday Review*. He died in 1990 — a full twenty-six years after being told by his doctor he wouldn't live to see Christmas.

It's impossible to tell, of course, whether Norman Cousin's recovery was solely due to Harpo's bicycle horn and Groucho's put-downs. He also took high does of vitamin C, was generally an optimistic person, and perhaps most importantly, left the hospital — somewhere he called "no place for a person who is seriously ill". But there's no doubt that laughter strengthens the immune system that fights disease, elevates the mood and releases positive emotions. And that can only be a good thing.

THE HEALING POWER OF MUSIC

Everything you've just learned about the healing power of laughter can be applied to music. A ton of research has been done indicating that regular listening to (or playing) music is a potent treatment for all kinds of health issues, including depression, stress, anxiety, chronic pain and even schizophrenia. As with laugher, sex, and meditation, music does this by producing positive physical and biological changes which boost the immune system, reduce heart rate, blood pressure and cortisol levels. Finally, there also appears to be a link between music, happiness and pleasure. Hearing songs that we like stimulates the same "pleasure center" of the brain that makes us laugh, quaff down our favorite foods, or snort a line of coke. Not that I'm advocating the latter, of course, but you get the picture. Music can be used as a drug. Only less expensive and better for you.

When choosing what music to listen to, I'd recommend sticking to upbeat tracks with a positive message. Create a playlist of your favorite feel-good tunes and incorporate listening to at least three tracks into your daily routine.

Below you'll find a collection of the best midlife crisis crushing songs I could find, curated from my own personal record collection.

MY "HELL YEAH!" PLAYLIST

YouTube: https://goo.gl/Gjgo68

Prescription: Turn volume up to ten. Dancing is optional, but recommended.

Warning: May create sudden feelings of happiness, renewed optimism and a lust for life. Use care when operating a car or dangerous machinery.

01. Beyond The Sea – Bobby Darin
02. There'll Be Some Changes Made – Dave Brubeck
03. Success – Iggy Pop
04. Time To Pretend – MGMT
05. Energy – The Apples In Stereo
06. Whatever It Is – Ben Lee
07. The Boss – James Brown
08. Come Back Brighter – Reef
09. Doing All Right – Queen
10. All We Have Is Now – The Flaming Lips
11. There's A New World Just Opening For Me – The Kinks

12. Winner Of The... – Pavement
13. Beginning To See The Light – The Velvet Underground
14. The Line Is Fine – Travis
15. It Doesn't Matter Anymore – The Supernaturals
16. Don't You Worry 'Bout A Thing – Stevie Wonder
17. On A Plain – Nirvana
18. Happiness – Elliott Smith
19. Lay Back In The Sun – Spiritualized
20. Some Sweet Day – Sparklehorse
21. You Get What You Give – New Radicals
22. This Will Be My Year – Semisonic
23. This Will Be Our Year – The Zombies
24. Movin' On Up – Primal Scream
25. We're A Winner – The Impressions
26. Road To Joy – Bright Eyes
27. Nothing'severgonnastandinmyway (again) – Wilco
28. Ola Kala – I'm From Barcelona
29. Mr. Lucky – John Lee Hooker
30. You Can Have The World – Cameo
31. I'm So Free – Lou Reed
32. A Change Is Gonna Come? – The High Fidelity
33. Ain't That A Kick In The Head – Dean Martin
34. Feel So Good – The Brian Jonestown Massacre
35. Hand In My Pocket – Alanis Morrisette
36. Sing A Happy Song – The O'Jays
37. Lucky Number Nine – The Moldy Peaches
38. Non, Je Ne Regrette Rien – Edith Piaf

39. All The Wine – The National

40. Things Are Looking Up – Fred Astaire

41. Younger Yesterday – The Polyphonic Spree

42. Mr Blue Sky – Electric Light Orchestra

43. Getting Better – The Beatles

44. Roll With It – Oasis

45. Solid – The Dandy Warhols

46. It Doesn't Matter – The Chemical Brothers

47. I'm Sitting On Top Of The World – Al Jolson

48. Don't Stop – Fleetwood Mac

49. I'm Blessed – Brendan Benson

50. Keep Your Sunny Side Up – Jane Gaynor

51. Feelin' All Right – Len

52. Beautiful – Carol King

53. Dry The Rain – The Beta Band

54. Paris Sous La Neige – Mellow

55. Whatever Will Be, Will Be (Que Sera Sera) – Doris Day

56. Vagabond – Wolfmother

57. Beautiful – Athlete

58. And When The Morning Comes – Superstar

59. You Take Yourself Too Seriously – The Supernaturals

60. Raindrops Keep Falling On My Head – Andy Williams

61. Do It All Over Again – Spiritualized

62. The Classical – Pavement

63. Love What You Do – The Divine Comedy

64. Consideration – Reef

65. Singin' In The Rain – Gene Kelly

66. Lady Day And John Coltrane – Gil Scott-Heron

67. Big Indian – The Dandy Warhols

68. Mr E's Beautiful Blues – Eels

69. Bad Days – The Flaming Lips

70. Lovely Day – Bill Withers

71. What A Wonderful World – Louis Armstrong

72. You Can't Always Get What You Want – The Rolling Stones

73. Good Times Comin' My Way – The Lassie Foundation

74. The 59th Bridge Song (Feeling Groovy) – Simon & Garfunkel

75. Move On Up – Curtis Mayfield

76. Float On – Modest Mouse

77. Hey Man (Now You're Really Living) – Eels

78. Always Look On The Bright Side Of Life – Monty Python

79. Don't Worry, Be Happy – Bobby McFerrin

80. Baby, I'm A Star – Prince

81. Smile – Nat "King" Cole

82. Don't Stop Me Now – Queen

83. O-o-h Child – Nina Simone

84. Beautiful – Christina Aguilera

85. Everything Is AWESOME!!! – Lego Movie

86. Mother, We Just Can't Get Enough – New Radicals

87. I'm So Glad – Cream

88. You Can Have It All – Yo La Tengo

89. Almost There – Lab Partners

90. It's Gettin' Better (Man!!) – Oasis

* * *

DIG DEEPER

Laughter Yoga – If you're that way inclined, why not join a laughter club?: https://www.meetup.com/laughteryoga/

The Top 100+ Funniest Movies of All Time – In need of inspiration for funny movies to watch? This list is a great place to start: http://www.rd.com/funny-stuff/the-top-100-funniest-movies-of-all-time/

The Funniest Interview You Will Ever See – Make a YouTube playlist of videos like this one to instantly lift your mood first thing in the morning: https://www.youtube.com/watch?v=hSFWgKI-O-A

Anatomy Of An Illness – Interview with Norman Cousins in which he discusses how he beat his disease through the power of laughter: https://www.youtube.com/watch?v=mqLAcpXzNks

Laugh With Me Session – Bianca Spears half hour laughter yoga video: https://www.youtube.com/watch?v=wtoXb6_oxck

STEP TWELVE

CHOOSE HAPPINESS

"What I used to be will pass away, and then you'll see that all I want now is happiness for you and me."
– Elliott Smith

I can safely say that the following three exercises were the ones that really helped me seal the deal in beating my midlife crisis. I had been going through a back-and-forth period of feeling better about things, and then not so good, but these exercises really killed off any lingering feelings of unhappiness, disappointment and regret still knocking around in my head. I hope they do the same for you.

PART ONE: MAKE A COMMITMENT

This may sound too simple to be effective, but you need to actually make a conscious commitment to forgo all of the negative emotions that have built up inside you — stress, anxiety, judgment, anger, etc. — in favor of happiness. It's time to simply choose happiness. By this I mean that you need to decide that from this day on, that you're going to really try to just look at the positive side of your life, rather than the negative. Focus on the fact that you're here, alive and on what you've got rather than what you haven't. I realize this may sound too simple and maybe similar to what you've already been told along the lines of "just get over it", but this is different. It's different if you consider that how we choose to think about all of our situations in life goes a long way to determining how we actually cope with them.

Now is the time to just let it go and be more like the duck I mentioned in the beginning of this book. Learn to shake the water off your back, and move on.

This takes perseverance, of course, but here's what I want you to do: type out your commitment on a piece of paper and tack it to the wall above a computer, kettle, mirror, or wherever you're likely to see it numerous times throughout the day. It might say something like "From this day forward I am going to look at the positive in life rather than the negative". Repeatedly saying this to yourself whenever you see it, will help keep you focused and on track with your goal. Here are two other practical steps you can do every day that will help you get there.

PART TWO: MORNING EXERCISE

Every morning from now on, I want you to do the following three things when you wake up:

Read your personal statement about what a great guy you are
Watch a two minute video that you find hilarious
Listen to a feel-good track
Think about how great you've got it

Here are some random thoughts I've gotten into the habit of thinking every morning:

It's amazing that I'm even alive. I should really make the most of this golden opportunity rather than complain about it.
I have XYZ going for me [my wife, friends, family, health, job or whatever it is].
How can my so-called problems be looked at as opportunities?
What do I really have to be unhappy about?

PART THREE: NIGHT EXERCISE

Furthering on from that exercise, every night before you go to bed, I want you to now do the following:

Make a list of three things that went well, or you enjoyed, or brought a smile to your face during the day. (It's best to write them down rather than simply think about them.) Just jot down three things which brought a smile to your face, whether they were big or small. They don't have to be out of the ordinary, amazing things like "I bumped into [insert favorite movie star's name] walking down the street." Rather, put down the simple things that made you happy in a small way like "I had an amazing slice of cake at Starbucks." Or "I had a great, funny conversation with Suzy this afternoon about UFOs."

The point of this is to begin to recalibrate your mind into appreciating the smaller things in life again, whether they involve your partner or not. In fact, both the morning and night exercises are designed to do just that — make you see that what you have is actually pretty amazing, if you'd only stop to think about it once in a while, rather than obsessing over "negative" things.

Do both exercises morning and night for two weeks and see how you feel by the end of it. I can guarantee you'll soon feel so much better than you do now, because this opportunity you have — every moment of this life — it's too good to waste on negativity.

THANK YOU!

Firstly, I want to say that I really appreciate you purchasing this book. Hopefully you feel a little better having just read it this first time. You've had to take a lot of information while reading it and, as you've probably noticed, a midlife crisis can be a difficult beast to pin down. Not only that but I've also thrown a lot of different theories at you regarding the ego, thoughts and emotions, free will and so on. Some may resonate with you more than others, but that's okay. See which steps make the most sense to you and focus on them.

It may take a week, it may take a month, it may take several months, but by following this program your repetitive thoughts, negativity and patterns of behavior *will* begin to dissipate. Your midlife crisis is not as strong as you think. All it takes is a little reframing of your thoughts and it will start to crumble.

Always remember…
As much as people might like to make us believe, being middle-aged is far from being "old".

You have so much to look forward to.

Onward!
Jeff Billings

PS: I'd love to hear any feedback or suggestions you might have on the book. Let me know what you think of it, and how it helped you nullify your midlife issues by emailing me at hello@manvsmidlifecrisis.com.

Midlife crisis in men

Made in the USA
Columbia, SC
26 October 2021